Democracy's Open Door

The Community College in America's Future

Marlene Griffith
Ann Connor

Boynton/Cook Publishers
HEINEMANN
Portsmouth, NH

Boynton/Cook Publishers, Inc.
A subsidiary of Reed Publishing (USA) Inc.
361 Hanover Street, Portsmouth, NH 03801-3912
Offices and agents throughout the world

Library of Congress Cataloging-in-Publication Data

Griffith, Marlene.
    Democracy's open door : the community college in America's future
/ Marlene Griffith, Ann Connor.
        p.   cm.
    Includes bibliographical references.
    ISBN 0-86709-330-7
    1. Community colleges—United States.   2. Education, Higher—
United States—Aims and objectives.   I. Connor, Ann.   II. Title.
LB2328.15.U6G75   1994
378'.052'0973—dc20   93-36836
                                                                  CIP

Editor: Peter R. Stillman
Production: Renée M. Pinard
Cover design: Lissa Seminara
Back cover photo: Ben Bagdikian

Printed in the United States of America on acid-free paper
98 97 96 95 94   CM   1 2 3 4 5 6 7 8 9

For Ben and for Devin

Contents

Foreword

Democracy's Open Door is a book with a passionate idea at its core, and the people in it speak with great passion. And the reader will hear many people speak, for, true to the democratic orientation of the book, Marlene Griffith and Ann Connor build an argument through the voices of others: community college students, tutors, teachers, and administrators. What these people say, our country needs to hear—that the community college provides opportunity to many with limited opportunity, that its success must be measured by broad-based democratic criteria—for over the last mean-spirited decade we have witnessed the diminishment of educational opportunity for all those except the privileged, the person prepared for standard achievement, the fast-track student.

The typical community college has a broad mission, broader than any other kind of American postsecondary institution: it offers collegiate courses providing access to four-year colleges and universities; it offers so-called "remedial" courses enabling underprepared students to gain access to further schooling; it offers basic courses in English which function as pathways to fuller participation in the society; it offers a range of occupational courses and programs, thereby enhancing employment possibilities; it offers general education courses and public service courses for the community at large. And the typical community college serves a broad, inclusive constituency: students headed toward the baccalaureate and students headed toward a technical occupation, students with limited resources, older students, working people, people who are venturing back into education, people displaced by economic restructuring, and people desperate to change the job they have. You'll hear from all these people in *Democracy's Open Door.*

Between them, Griffith and Connor have worked in the community college for almost fifty years, and they combine this experience with the experience of others in community colleges across the country to celebrate the mission of this American innovation. It would be hard to come away from this book without some reflection on what it means to have an open educational system. But what Griffith and Connor do as well (and this is exceedingly important) is argue that the criteria most often used to judge the community college — criteria drawn from evaluation studies of research universities and four-year colleges, from flawed life-span development models, from traditional images of academic success — are unsound and inappropriate and lead to harsh, damaging assessment, from academicians and policy analysts, from the political right and left. Griffith and Connor call for a better, richer measure.

I remember driving with a friend of mine through economically depressed East Los Angeles a few years back and passing the local community college. He had gone there, as had many of his friends. "You know," he said, "that place was the only chance we had. We would have been lost without it." The passionate idea at the core of *Democracy's Open Door* is that educational opportunity means access and access means local, open, and specific institutional pathways, pathways originating in communities, serving communities, measured by the degree to which they provide members of a community with the possibility of a better life.

Mike Rose
Los Angeles, 1993

Acknowledgments

This book would not have been written had it not been for the thousands of students who entered our lives over the years, and invited us to enter their lives, as we went about teaching at two California community colleges. Our students, whose experiences in higher education so often remain unacknowledged, inspired us to write about the importance of community colleges in the making of individual lives

Nor could we have written this book without the many people who graciously consented to be interviewed on tape. Their generosity with time, their patience and openness in letting us understand their experiences and thinking about community colleges and students were invaluable. We invariably came away with new ideas, fresh perspectives, entertaining anecdotes, and a sense of optimism about the many good people involved in community college work. Unfortunately, we couldn't use all the words of all of the people. A list of whom we interviewed and here acknowledge is at the end of the text.

We are grateful to friends, some teachers, some not, who read various versions of the manuscript and offered us valuable suggestions: Francine Foltz, Sandra Gilbert, Gerald Kohs, Dorothea Nudelman, Margaret Ralston, Marian Robinson, Susan Schacher, Peggy Webb, and Alison Wilson. Barbara Bilson and Katherine Fulton helped us set up interviews in Santa Monica, California, and Durham, North Carolina. Alma Oberst Holmgren, Roderick Holmgren, Lou R. Russell, and Smokey Wilson conducted interviews for us in Kentucky, Colorado, North Carolina, and Wyoming.

In addition to reading several chapters, Patricia Cross offered us valuable suggestions on research material. Smokey

Wilson's close reading raised many questions, and her ongoing conversations helped focus Chapter 6. Nicholas F. Keefe was an important resource who kept us current on the latest developments in vocational education. And Robert J. Griffin's ready blue pencil made us hear what we had written in new ways.

We thank Jack Hailey, our agent, who understood the book right away; and Peter Stillman, our editor, who shepherded it to publishable form. At Heinemann, Cheryl Kimball stood behind us all the way, and Renée Pinard transformed the manuscript into a book with humane efficiency.

Finally, we are warmly appreciative of Mike Rose, who believed in the book enough to offer us a foreword. And we are well aware of the debt we owe Ben Bagdikian, who encouraged us throughout, kept us working, and was there always when we needed him.

Introduction

We have written this book because we are worried about the hundreds of community colleges in America. We are worried about what will happen to them as state after state cuts funds to higher education and as enrollments increase — a trickle-down effect from four-year colleges and universities suffering their own cutbacks. We are worried that what may be destroyed is the egalitarian vision shared by these colleges — the Open Door — a vision that knits them into the biggest and boldest system of higher education in the world.

The Open Door promises that every adult of whatever age is welcome to college without qualifying by virtue of high school grades, test scores, or previous cultural advantages. It is why a recent international commission called the community colleges in the United States "democracy's colleges." In this book, we keep students prominent in the picture because their characteristics range so widely that they differ from all other students in higher education.

In fact, the Open Door community college does precisely what national leaders say is desperately needed: it concentrates on the neglected first two years of college; it raises educational levels of underprepared students; it educates and trains students of all ages to be qualified, skilled workers; and it retrains and re-educates those whose skills are outdated, whose jobs have been lost, or who have college degrees but no work skills. It does all this with decades of past experience and at less than half the tuitions of other public institutions of higher education.

But today we see that door closing, slowly enough that it is hardly noticed except by those it affects. Tests are being devised to restrict enrollment. Tuitions are being increased.

Students are being asked to prove an ability to benefit before they can enroll. The time allowed them to enter or to finish a program is being shortened. Moreover, the different functions of the community college are being pitted against each other as, for example, remedial and job-training courses get cut to salvage the academic curriculum.

And so we write out of a sense of urgency. We write from within the system. Between us, we have worked in community colleges for forty-nine years, one on an inner city campus, one on a suburban campus. We know that keeping the door open for some but slowly closing it for others will have disastrous effects on the many functions of these colleges; it will undermine the most democratic achievement of American higher education.

Because most community colleges are comprehensive in nature — offering transfer, vocational, remedial, and general education programs, and community activities — they are flexible enough to respond quickly to changes in the educational needs of their local communities. They offer a second, or even third, chance to those who need it. They accommodate part-timers, students who work, students who need child care, and those students who take a few classes, drop out (or, more accurately, "stop out"), and then return, perhaps shifting direction as their own needs and the country's civic, cultural, and employment patterns change.

These colleges are what their name says they are — colleges centered in the communities that surround them, within commuting distance of home and work. They build local bridges to the culture of learning, to the culture of work, to the culture of the larger community. They are dedicated to the discovery and development of human potential, often the potential of people whose abilities have been overlooked, people who have been passed over or passed along.

THIS UNIQUE EDUCATIONAL system is threatened because it suffers from a whole series of public and professional misunderstandings and misperceptions that measure its functions, its achievements, and the success of its students by standards that do not apply. Ironically, it is just now becoming visible to those debating educational policy.

It is urgent for America to understand that community colleges need to stay multi-functional. People both inside and outside community colleges must understand what these institutions do, what unique role they fill in higher education. Otherwise, we fear that under the pressure of dwindling funds and increasing numbers of students, community colleges will be altered, arbitrarily, without recognition that they are a part of the American educational system that works, an open door for a new breed of students who now need and demand higher education — older men and women of all racial and ethnic backgrounds, part-time students who must work, who view education as a life-long endeavor, who return to campuses again and again as their lives, their goals, and their culture change.

And so:

- We urge policymakers at all levels to recognize the uniqueness of the Open Door community colleges and to work to maintain their comprehensiveness, their low cost, and their ability to accommodate students who are learning on their own terms and in their own time.
- We urge those involved in community college education to recognize their significant role as agents of change: from a society that is widening the gap between educational and economic haves and have-nots to a society where all doors are open to all people.
- We urge parents and high school counselors to be aware of the educational opportunities community colleges offer their children.
- We urge more businesses and industries to collaborate with community colleges in establishing classes and programs which provide renewable training and education.
- And we urge local citizens to support community college policymakers who are dedicated to the broad missions of

these colleges, not a return to the "good old days" of junior colleges.

We hope that this book will demonstrate the value of Open Door institutions of higher learning, and to convince the reader that this uniquely American institution may have an even more critical role in the years ahead.

One

The New Educational Reality

I am particularly interested in knowing more about efforts to reduce geographic and economic barriers to the development of individual talents through extended educational opportunities which seem to be reflected in many states and localities by so-called "community colleges." It is apparent that various patterns are being followed and that an important educational development is being undertaken through trial, adaptation, and democratic experimentation.

— Harry S. Truman, 1950

*I*n the current national debate about higher education, millions of words and scores of reports are based on the wrong assumption, the assumption that most American college students follow a linear educational path. They are most frequently imagined as eighteen-year-olds enrolling in a four-year college, graduating when they are twenty-two, and then taking up professional life, or perhaps going to graduate school.

In fact, statistically and in the lives of a majority of Americans who attend institutions of higher education, that assumption is false. Nearly half the students enrolled in public higher education are not in conventional four-year colleges, and they are not all eighteen to twenty-two years old.

Nearly six million American adults are enrolled in community college credit courses (those that count toward degrees and certificates). Two-thirds attend part-time. Most of these students work. Their average age is twenty-nine. Many of them do not follow a straight path toward a clearly defined academic goal. Instead, their educational lives zig and zag. They leave school to take a job or have a baby or reorganize their lives; they come back, perhaps with a different goal, a different attitude, once, twice, three times.

"This pattern of ad hoc attendance seems to fit the desires expressed and demonstrated by students who are using the colleges for their own purposes," say two friendly critics of the community college, Arthur M. Cohen and Florence B. Brawer. Whether it's called zigzagging or ad hoc attendance, the pattern of students attending college and setting and achieving academic goals in their own way and time is one that is most often seen in community colleges, but increasingly is also in evidence at four-year colleges. At community colleges, the practice is so prevalent that students who stop coming are no longer called drop-outs; the term now in use is stop-outs. In order to offer "extended educational opportunities," community colleges have learned to deal with the personal and social realities in the lives of their students.

Consider Connie Brown. White, middle-class, now in her mid-thirties, an assistant head nurse in a major hospital and a home-owner, Connie attended three community colleges over a period of fifteen years before earning her RN certificate at the last of them.

Or David Mullen. African American, from a drug and crime-ridden community, David attended two different community colleges before and after Navy service, entered a four-year state college, left after two semesters and returned to a community college so that he could reorder his personal and financial life. Eventually, at age thirty-two, he earned a baccalaureate degree. For the past five years he has been working in a bookstore and tutoring, and is now in graduate school, getting ready for a teaching career.

Connie and David first started college as soon as they finished high school, but many students don't begin until they are in their mid-twenties or mid-thirties or even older. Their numbers include not only veterans but new immigrants, women who want to enter the workforce, workers who need to upgrade or change job skills, senior citizens who never before had a chance at higher education, as well as younger adults who simply felt the need to get out of the classroom for awhile after high school.

It is not out of the ordinary for students to move in and out of institutions of higher education for ten, fifteen, twenty years or even longer. And often each move, each zig or zag, reflects a slightly changed goal—to gain entry to middle-class life and careers, to change or upgrade jobs, to find richer and fuller lives.

There are reasons for this new educational reality. The nature of the American economy has become so fluid and dynamic that of necessity students select the educational resources that fit their and society's needs at a particular moment. But their and society's needs change. By the year 2000, for example, the U. S. Department of Labor projects that workers will have as many as three careers and seven different jobs in their lifetimes, that three-fourths of all jobs will require postsecondary education, and that more than five-sixths of those entering the workforce will be minorities, women, and immigrants.

Once it is understood that a zigzag educational path can benefit both students and society, the public community college emerges as a central institution.

PUBLIC COMMUNITY COLLEGES number nearly one thousand, depending on who does the counting, and exist in every state except South Dakota (where there are three tribally controlled two-year colleges). They are open to virtually all, and geographically convenient. More than ten million students are enrolling in community colleges, nearly six million in college credit courses and at least five million in non-credit courses. The cost per term is, on the national average, less than half (forty-three percent) that of public four-year institutions, although it varies by state.

And yet the public community college is almost never mentioned by those who propose or direct national public policy. In recent years there has been nothing as dramatic as the interest of President Harry S. Truman or the support of Truman's Commission on Higher Education. That was more than forty years ago.

Today, neither the American public in general nor those especially concerned with education fully comprehend the reality and the potential of the community college. Most middle-class, college-oriented people see these colleges, if they see them at all, as deficient imitations of "real" colleges or as training schools. Only a dim perception exists of their multiple functions and their importance to national life. We want to make visible the real characteristics of this remarkable network of higher education and to document its importance as the country reshapes its educational and workforce policies.

Invisibility creates vulnerability. Political and budgetary pressures threaten to turn comprehensive community colleges into much narrower institutions, serving younger, perhaps better prepared students who have traditional collegiate goals which they can pursue with few interruptions. Such a transformation, we argue, would be a national tragedy. It would not only ignore the ordinary people in thousands of communities for whom these colleges become the lifeline to a better life; it would also ignore the needs of industries and other businesses, in every region, for upgraded skills training on a large scale.

And that introduces the second major theme developed in this book: that the public community college as an institution is especially relevant during the 1990s. The much talked about changes in technology demand that people continually be able to alter their skills. The need for this kind of evolution and transformation of the American workforce is enunciated regularly from the President on down, but rarely do we hear anything about the mechanisms for such transformation.

American community colleges are one of the chief mechanisms, but the critical role they can play in this decade remains veiled. To be sure, it takes vigilance to assure that the economic needs within communities do not overwhelm the educational potential for individuals. The multiple offerings of the colleges and the zigzag patterns open to students provide some necessary safety valves.

WE WRITE AS two women who went back to school with very limited funds when we were over thirty. One, a single mother of two preschoolers, had been a journalist; the other wanted to change from office work to teaching. We were educated, middle-class women; we re-entered at the university level, but we learned firsthand what it feels like to change direction and start in again.

The start, then, the foundation, of this book is our personal and professional experiences. Both of us taught English courses, from basic skills to Shakespeare. In addition, one of us co-founded and taught in an entry program for severely underprepared students; the other administered an off-campus program serving nearly ten thousand students in locations as varied as a Hewlett-Packard plant, a Navy base, a senior center. Beyond that, we have studied the history and evolution of the community college "system," we have read widely on community college issues, and we have read widely on other educational and social issues and trends. We have also interviewed students, faculty, administrators; we listened to real people telling the untold stories of their colleges and their educational lives. Listening to these stories reinforced what we had known intuitively from our own experiences and seen confirmed by national patterns and statistics. Community college students fit few media images and few personal images of "student." They attend on a different time line; their lives move to a different rhythm.

These students rarely find a place in public imagery. Self images, however, are often shaped as much by shared public imagery as by personal experience. It was not unusual to find such a student as Connie, who, in retrospect, felt good about her learning and her achievements, but apologetic about her pathway. Few of us point with pride to the student whose undergraduate education zigzags along for ten or fifteen years, especially when that student is oneself.

The traditional linear mode works well for many students, but no longer for most who need access to institutions of higher education. The point here is not that one pathway is preferable. The point is that American higher education offers a unique variety of pathways that are crucial to the lives of contemporary students and to the health of contemporary society. Ironically only one of these — the linear route through the four-year school — is validated in public imagery, public discourse, or public consciousness.

Why is this so? One reason is the survival of outdated assumptions about and imagery of college students. Even when they are no longer seen as frolicking on beaches during spring break, they are still viewed as young people living in dorms and pursuing their studies full time. The public needs to broaden this image to include the many contemporary students who extend their undergraduate education long past the conventional four to five years.

A second reason, closely connected, is that community college students often arrive from outside the circles of success or high ambition. Like David, they may come from the lower half of the social and economic spectrum — although this is beginning to change now that four-year college costs are rising above the reach of even middle-class families — or like Connie, they may come from bland, underachieving high school careers.

Community colleges are *deliberately inclusive*. Their student bodies are demographically representative of the communities in which the colleges are located. Their students certainly include middle-class students. But they also include working-class people, first generation immigrants, reentry women, poor people — the Americans we rarely see in advertisements or in movies or in sitcoms, the Americans who are rarely targeted for readership by magazines or newspapers, the invisible members of society. In this book we try to make these

6

colleges and all their students visible, and broaden the national image of college students to include men and women like David and Connie. But we also broaden the discussion on higher education to include a close look at how adult students construct their own educational patterns.

In recent years, public educational debate has been dominated by men like Allan Bloom, who sampled students "of the kind who populate the twenty or thirty best universities" and found them lacking; in *The Closing of the American Mind*, he offers as "the only serious solution ... the good old Great Books approach." University faculties continue to be wrenched by often acrimonious debates over the "canon," that is, over what books should be taught in undergraduate literature and core courses. In different ways, all are concerned about curriculum and texts, with what a course should offer and to whom.

Within some educational circles, there is talk about what goes on inside the classroom, about the place of the lecture class versus the small seminar, for instance, or about the interactions between student and teacher. But only rarely is the focus on *how* students use or are hindered by what they are offered. On *how* they use their education to build their lives.

A certain coherence comes only with hindsight when experience is recollected in tranquillity. Throughout this book, men and women who have studied at community colleges reflect on how and why this phase of their education has affected their lives and the lives of those around them. David, for example, in Chapter 2, shows us in ways we could not possibly have perceived except through his eyes that community colleges serve as a "middle ground between what is really going on in the community and what is happening in individual lives of the people who live within the community."

In letting men and women who study and work at these institutions talk in their own voices, we hope to show how community colleges are changing the social fabric by letting ordinary people write new educational scripts for themselves.

7

Two

David and Connie: Writing Their Own Educational Scripts

Our lives not only take new directions; they are subject to repeated redirection.

— Mary Catherine Bateson, *Composing a Life*

If you had walked into Cody's bookstore on Telegraph Avenue in Berkeley in the early nineties, you might have seen David Mullen at a checkout register near the door, talking to customers about their purchases as he rings up sales. David is an African American in his mid-thirties, dark, handsome. He has a neat appearance and an easy way with people. He worked all over the store, depending on the need: shelving books, using a computer to help identify and locate books, unpacking books in the back room. He also was responsible for ordering books for the sections on Africa, Film and Media, Music, Sports, and all books by African American writers. David has always liked to read, liked to be around books, and sometimes fantasized about starting a bookstore in Oakland specializing in books by African American authors.

We meet David for lunch at a coffee shop next to the book store, and he talks about a film script he's writing, about the possibility of going to graduate school and qualifying for a teaching credential. And he talks about how he got where he is today. "If the community college didn't exist, I probably wouldn't have made it," he says.

His background includes many of the ills that now are threatening the nation's life: poverty, drugs, crime, minority status, lack of employment opportunities, lack of hope. David made it by taking a circuitous path that accommodated three enrollments in two community colleges, and two tries at a state university; it took him twelve years to earn a baccalaureate degree. Five years beyond that B.A., he describes his experiences with critical distance.

"When I first started going to college," he says, "I had no idea what I was doing. I did pretty much everything off the cuff, didn't have a set plan to get from point A to point B, didn't really know what point A and point B were. I just knew I wanted to write and college should be able to help me do that.

"There are a lot of people out there who are like the first generation of their families to go to college, and there's no one at home to give them any advice, any guidance, or whatever, so they are strictly making this up on the run." David is talking about himself.

"A lot of people just have this longing, and at one point in their life say OK, I want to go for something better, and they're not sure how to do it, but there's this college, it's down the street, it doesn't cost much, so they go there."

David began at a community college down the street. At the time he was living with his mother in Compton, a drug-plagued town adjacent to Los Angeles, which he describes as "having the worst gang crime in the country, worse than Harlem, worse than Watts." (When he had moved to Oakland, he moved a younger brother out of Compton so he wouldn't die doing drugs or get killed in gang warfare.) He first majored in business and computers because he was told it was a good field, but then he decided that "if I was going to work so hard at something it might as well be something I liked, so I switched my major to journalism." His dream was to be a writer, but "reality just drifted along. It was a major step to switch from business to journalism, a first attempt to bring the two together, [to move] from what I wanted to do to what I was doing."

9

After two semesters, he enlisted in the Navy rather than wait to be drafted. Discharged, he did not return to Compton, but settled in Oakland where he had relatives. His Aunt Minnie was taking classes off and on at Oakland's Laney College, so David decided to enroll there too. The next couple of years were good for David. He took courses in creative writing and journalism, along with basic requirements, and he became a tutor in the college writing center for underprepared students. He also worked off-campus. He now remembers that "I was always tired and didn't have enough time. I hated working and I loved going to school."

David succeeded at Laney. When he first started taking community college classes, "it was like all eyes were on me . . . ; everyone was watching me because I was the only one doing it; I was the only one who was really going to college, trying to make it work, trying to be successful at it." When he graduated, he says, "everyone was really impressed. My mother came up from LA, and my grandfather came." And he set an example for several members of his family who later enrolled in community college programs, like his Aunt Minnie and a cousin.

It had taken him three years at Laney to accumulate the credits he needed to be accepted, as a junior, at San Francisco State University. David was twenty-seven years old when he moved to San Francisco and started taking classes, but that first try did not work out. "I was completely demoralized at San Francisco State. I couldn't get a part-time job. My expenses were much higher than they had been in Oakland and my car broke down. Plus I had to deal with this attitude. I really was a down and outer, and I was with these students, 'we are the haves and you are the have-nots,' and that made it a lot worse.

"I was going to summer school and the VA messed up my records. The rent was due, I didn't have any food, and I find out that I haven't been processed for summer school and it would be three months before I'd have a check, so I said, well forget it. . . . I decided I really didn't need to get my bachelor's degree anyway; I'll just get a job and do something else."

David moved back to Oakland and the cultural comfort zone offered by Laney.

To make ends meet, he took on a part-time job at an all-night newspaper stand and bookstore in downtown Oakland. But more importantly, he again enrolled in courses and in addition, for twenty hours a week at $5.25 an hour, he worked as a writing and reading tutor in basic skill classes at the college. He says of that time in his life, "I sort of remembered what I could do and what I wanted, what it took to get it. It was like getting recharged."

Two years later he went for his second try at San Francisco State University, but this time he "was ready for it." He kept his apartment in Oakland, and he continued to work as a tutor at Laney. "So I'd go to Laney in the morning and tutor classes, and in the afternoon I'd go to San Francisco State to my classes, and that sort of kept me going."

It's easy to underestimate the stress on the pioneer, including the pioneer in academic culture. The experiences and challenges for the Davids are far different from those for students whose families are involved in their education or who are going to college because all their friends are going to college. What does it take to enter a new world where one feels like a stranger while struggling with daily living problems that are exhausting and create tensions?

"You need more nurture," David says now. "And a community college provides that environment, and the nurturing comes almost automatically because that's what happens when people are in the same struggle together. They try to help each other." It may be that David's decision to take on a heavy tutoring load—becoming part of that nurturing—helped recharge his will and motivation. Perhaps we all need to retouch base, to reassure ourselves that what we set out to do is worth doing.

Not all experiences are as positive as David's, but community colleges across the country are noted for providing a supportive springboard from which to move. While community college faculties are proud of that fact, the fact also is used to criticize community colleges for not being rigorous enough. David's experience knocks a sizable hole in this argument.

When we talk about community college students zigzagging through higher education, writing new educational scripts for themselves, we mean students like David who, as he says, "never took the SAT and never took any college prep courses in high school," students who do not follow predictable patterns. But we also mean students like Connie Brown who is the oldest daughter in a highly educated middle-class family; her father is a college professor; her now-deceased mother was a medical social worker.

We didn't go to Connie's workplace to find her because she works the 4 P.M. to midnight shift at a large hospital, where she's assistant head nurse on an oncology floor. We met for tea on one of her days off. And we couldn't help being impressed with this attractive, dark-haired young woman and where she is now. Like David, she's in her mid-thirties; she was recently married and she and her husband are buying a house. She feels centered in her life, and you just know she's the kind of person you'd want to be your nurse if you were hospitalized.

But Connie spent a lot of time "floating around, not sure what I was going to do" before she achieved personal and professional success. She graduated from a Pasadena high school in June and started at Pasadena City College that fall. "I was always told that I was so bright, and that I had such a high IQ, that I was intelligent, and that I just had to apply myself. I guess I thought I would transfer to Berkeley, to a four-year college, but that wasn't clear.

"It took me all sorts of courses to find out what I was really interested in. It took quite a while. I took theater courses, and at the same time I thought, oh, I want to go to medical school, which was pie-in-the-sky, because my grades had been kind of average in high school, and I hadn't gone right into college and started taking math and science. I just wasn't sure what I wanted to do with my life."

Connie didn't begin to find out what it was she wanted until she moved to Northern California "and worked at a kind of dead-end job in a restaurant in downtown Oakland. I realized that if I didn't go back to school and pursue something I'd be stuck in this restaurant with women who were sixty years old and were bitter about life and had been waitresses all their lives, and I thought if I don't do something, that's what I'll end up doing because I don't have any skills."

She was the fountain girl, the one who made all the banana splits. She now says "I think I learned a lot about work, what it means to go to a lousy job every day, to keep going, by working at that job. But then I realized that I had to get some sort of training if I wanted to be able to do other things than working in a restaurant. So I started at Laney then. I'd take theater classes which I was real interested in and made a lot of good friends, but I realized that theater is real competitive and I don't know if you can really make a good living in the field unless you're real talented. I still was taking all sorts of other general education courses and then I got into the licensed vocational nurse (LVN) program there."

It was not a straight and easy path. "I had thought about medical school, which was a fantasy — I had been interested in medicine and health — and LVN seemed like a program that would train me to be able to work. It took me longer than the usual eighteen months — I had sort of a crisis and didn't know if that was what I really wanted to do. The upshot was that I missed a lot of time, had to go an extra semester, but I finally did graduate from that program and took the state boards." She immediately started working at a local hospital.

"I think it took me ten years to decide to go back and get my RN. I worked for quite a while in nursing, as an LVN, and realized that if I didn't go back and upgrade, I would be sort of stuck at a certain level. I wouldn't have much choice or job mobility. That was something I had been struggling with for a long time, whether I wanted to go back to school. Considering my record and how it had been in the past, I had mixed feelings about school."

The RN program demanded science prerequisites and Connie had avoided science. "It was a real struggle for me to see it [an anatomy and physiology course] through. It was a hard course and I was so anxious about whether or not I'd be able to do it, but I did pretty well. I also took a microbiology course and got into a little study group with some other students and had a real good instructor who was concerned and interested and I remember when I got a B on the final I was so shocked! It was like a turning point."

After taking the science prerequisites, Connie was accepted into a RN program at a third community college. She went in as an advanced placement student because, with her LVN work experience, she was able to take exams to challenge the first year of the program. And, as she now says, she was "much more motivated. It was a real mixed program, not just eighteen-year-olds. There were a lot of people my age and older, some who had bachelor's degrees in other fields and who wanted to get into nursing. There were younger people, pretty much right out of high school. There were about five or six of us who had been LVNs, had worked in health care, and had come in as advanced placement students. For me it worked out really well."

Many parents, especially well-educated middle-class parents such as Connie's, would like their children to follow a more conventional path, get good grades in high school, go right through college. But not all of their children do that. Some more or less float around, seemingly unfocused, the way Connie did, or they get turned off by high school, become rebellious or simply determined to do their own thing. This is a very different student from the one who comes from a family where she or he may be the first even to consider college, where the family may be applying pressure not to continue schooling, to go to work instead, to help out at home, or where family members may be neither encouraging nor discouraging but simply unaware of what college means. For those students, like David, the act of going to college is a daring crossing of boundaries: not a holding back, but a risking ahead.

What students like David and Connie do share is this: as adults they found acceptance and direction at institutions that let them have a strong hand in writing their own educational scripts and creating their own educational time lines. There are, of course, institutional requirements for degree or certificate programs in all colleges, two-year as well as four-year. But for a large number of students like Connie and David, it is not peers or institutional patterns that determine how many courses they take, or when they interrupt, or come back. It is their own lives and needs.

This difference between the academically prepared and economically more affluent college-bound cohort and the millions outside this tradition highlights the importance of community colleges. They provide inexpensive education within commuting distance from home. They are open enough and flexible enough to let students of all ages work out educational patterns that are directly related to their lives. And they are flexible enough to respond to local populations and local economic demands and needs. The community ends up with more citizens who are self-supporting, pay taxes, buy houses, start businesses. Or, looked at from another angle, local industry and local services are assured a workforce geared to local needs.

In the world of the 1990s, our economic well-being, both as individuals and as a nation, is increasingly tied to education. Most new jobs will require at least some education past a high school diploma. What used to be a requirement for college entry is now being asked of applicants to entry level jobs: to be well-grounded in basic knowledge and to have an intellectual framework to which new knowledge can be added. Of the twenty million new workers who will enter the work force between now and the year 2000, eighty-two percent will be female, non-white, or immigrant. Access to continuing education and retraining is now a social necessity.

At the same time, the split between educational haves and have-nots is widening. Those with less education, less literacy, do not earn sufficient income for secure and productive lives. According to a 1989 census report, one out of four adults over twenty-five had not completed high school.

Chances are, they will earn less than $5000 a year. They are more likely to lose their jobs, and more apt to be on welfare, homeless on the streets, or in prison. Nearly sixty percent of prison inmates did not complete high school.

We have no way of knowing when or if students who take the occasional class, on and off, in and out, may find a direction that lets them become a Connie or a David. Or whether a Connie or a David will return after their first or second try. We have no records that track these interrupted paths over a period of years.

Could Connie have completed a health care program after her first two years at a community college? We doubt it. The work experience, the coming face to face with "women who were sixty years old and were bitter about life" provided a stepping stone that no one could have planned for her. Motivation and self-esteem may grow slowly. Could she have tackled two hard science courses before she had completed some less demanding courses, had eight years of successful work experience, worked out "some personal problems"? Again, probably not.

Connie's educational path took new directions as she was traveling it. It looked and it felt chaotic at the time, and as she says, "I knew it was distressing to my parents." And she still feels somewhat apologetic—"I've gone about this sort of backwards; I've just gone all these alternative routes; it's taken me all these years." Cultural expectations, like stereotypes, are strong.

When we asked her how she now views her first years at Pasadena City College—were they useful, we asked—she said, "I think I learned a lot in terms of basic general education. I took my English courses there, and philosophy, and American institutions. I still think of these people and a lot of them inspired me to go on and try other things. The couple of years I spent down there were real good years even though I was sort of floating around and not sure what I was going to do."

In the name of efficiency and cost-effectiveness, and because the zigzagging paths of many students are largely unacknowledged and invisible, new pressures from legisla-tures, budget committees, and sometimes from the colleges themselves are aiming to streamline the path. Students are given less time to find their way, to catch up. They are asked very quickly to name their goal and show proof that they are pursuing it, more quickly it seems than at the four-year school where students are traditionally allowed the first two years to "declare a major."

In no way are we arguing against better guidance within academic and vocational programs. Or against financial aid or other non-academic support which might keep students in college. But it is a dangerous fiction to assume that "normal" two-year or four-year education follows a linear and mostly uninterrupted path. On no level of education above junior high school is this true.

At community colleges nationally, the nineteen-year-olds are still the dominant single age group (both Connie and David were nineteen when they first attended). But the com-prehensive community college is unique in that it can serve the goal-directed nineteen-year-old at the same time that it continues to welcome the adult Connies and Davids, the stu-dents who are by now the majority in American education, who enroll and interrupt and re-enroll, and whose goals often define and redefine themselves in the process of their lives.

That, after all, is how people live and grow. In that way, community colleges allow, encourage, and support students working their way through school in more ways than one.

Three

Community College Students: Diverse Goals, Diverse Paths

A careful observer of the community college scene is impressed by the remarkably broad spectrum of human beings to be found there. This comprehensive nature of the community college is an aspect of American education most difficult to interpret to visitors from abroad.

— Edmund J. Gleazer, Jr., 1988

*S*andra Acebo, a community college teacher and administrator, talking to us about what the community college is all about and who it is for, tells a story about Miami-Dade Community College, where she once interned for its president, Robert McCabe.

"McCabe has this famous speech that he gives; the staff even kid about it now because he tells the story so often, and you can almost see when he's getting worked up to tell the story. They call it his *Viva America* story.

"McCabe loves graduation," Acebo continues. "Everybody shows up, Mom and Pop, Grandma and Grandpa, and everybody in the family. They all show up. McCabe was at one graduation and it had been a very long ceremony because there were so many to go up and get the diplomas, and when students walked up on the stage to get diplomas, there'd be clapping and cheering. But when this one Hispanic student went up to get his diploma, a guy at the very back of the gym, way, way up on the bleachers, stood up and waved his arms, and yelled 'Viva America!'"

According to Acebo, McCabe uses the story to illustrate the mission of community colleges. That's what we are here for, he says. That's what we are here to do, to give people a chance who otherwise wouldn't have a chance, and to give them a second chance, and to give them a third chance: that's our function.

For McCabe and Acebo, who now is Vice-President of Instruction at DeAnza College in Cupertino, California, and for many other community college administrators and faculty, this is their overriding, if unofficial, function. To quote Acebo: "We can take people who otherwise would disappear as far as their own sense of self-worth and the contribution they can make to their families and their communities, and we can help those people along."

Officially speaking, however, in mission statements and catalogs, most community colleges describe their multiple functions differently:

- To offer collegiate courses so that students can transfer, as juniors, to four-year colleges or universities.
- To offer occupational or career programs geared to local employment opportunities.
- To provide what are called general education courses, courses which offer knowledge for personal and civic life.
- To offer remedial courses which prepare students for college-level work and, for those who need it, offer special tutors and other support.
- To offer a variety of cultural, recreational, and business-oriented public services to the community at large, such as non-credit (and usually pay-as-you-go) courses, lecture series, book fairs, museum activities, music and drama festivals, recreational swimming and other sports activities, business advisory centers.

These specific functions developed as junior colleges matured into complex community colleges and State and Federal accountants had a need to establish service classifications for funding purposes. Other categories developed: full-time students, part-time students; day students, evening students; matriculated students, non-matriculated students; credit students, non-credit students. Bureaucratic needs aside, these functional categories are useful in making concrete the idea that community colleges are comprehensive in nature and serve many diverse populations. But, somewhat paradoxically, it would be a mistake to think that every student fits neatly into a single category; in fact, many students straddle the lines of demarcation, fitting into more than one category simultaneously, moving back and forth across category lines.

The student in the white lab coat wearing an identification tag indicating enrollment in a respiratory therapy program may also be taking classes which would transfer to a four-year institution; the student enrolled in a remedial math class may also be taking a sociology class leading to the two-year associate degree; the night student may sometimes attend day classes; the full-time student this term may attend only part time another term; the student in a non-credit class may also be a credit student.

The fact that students need not squeeze themselves into a single category provides occupational, academic, and personal mobility for large numbers of American adults. Moreover, they also may be doing well in classes and stop attending for a while, perhaps to digest, discard, shift direction, and then return. Recent surveys confirm that the attendance behaviors of students are more dependent on their personal lives, their job lives, the outside world, than on anything happening within the college. Remember Cohen and Brawer's comment that "this pattern of ad hoc attendance seems to fit the desires expressed and demonstrated by students who are using the colleges for their own purposes." It may also, of course, meet important needs of the society they're part of.

The first chance, second chance, third chance opportunities in which community colleges take such pride depend, however, on the many different courses and programs offered in one place, on their multiple functions. Take, for example,

Patricia Keller, now a lawyer in private practice, who was a part-time student, a full-time student, a general education student, and a transfer student — all at the same college, and, in her case, during an uninterrupted course of study. At age eighteen, Patricia never had a chance to go to college. Her mother had a fifth-grade education, and, according to Patricia, "she thought she was doing well supporting me by herself to see me through high school. So there were no expectations from my family to go on. I married right out of high school."

She was in the furniture business with her husband for two decades, "but I wasn't the guiding light in that business; I played an ancillary role." She also had two children, and "one hundred percent of my life energy was going out toward my family." Then her husband decided to retire from his business and the children were in school, "and that left me with time on my hands." She lived near a community college and decided to sign up for some classes. She took general education courses, interior design, and then ceramics, attending as a part-time student. Then a counselor suggested that she enroll in classes leading to an associate of arts (A.A.) degree. "I was scared. I just had no confidence in myself. But when I attended classes, that was pure pleasure. I caught fire."

Patricia got her A.A. degree and transferred to a four-year university to obtain a B.A. She later received a law degree, passed the bar, and now is in private practice. The community college "gave me the confidence to go on," she now says. It also let her move, cautiously, from being a part-time student who was taking random courses of interest, to becoming a full-time student working toward an associate degree, and taking mostly (but not all) transfer courses, all within one institution that had become familiar and supportive.

Or consider Elaine Dormshield, who had earned a baccalaureate degree in International Relations from Stanford University, but had no real work skills. "I had been a housewife for four or five years and had recently gotten divorced." She entered a community college as a "reverse transfer" student, a category for an increasing number of older students with college degrees but no work skills, or, given the current employment picture, out-of-date or inappropriate skills.

Elaine was a part-time student for a year, taking biology and anatomy/physiology. "At Stanford," she said, "my science was geology." These were officially "transfer" courses but Elaine enrolled in order to be accepted into a vocational program in Respiratory Therapy as a full-time student. She now is employed as an administrator at a large hospital.

In Wisconsin, Joe D. too had been to a university before he enrolled in a community college, but unlike Elaine, he did not get a degree. He dropped out. Eventually he enrolled in the Madison Area Technical College which also offers general education courses leading to an associate degree. There his "bad study habits" tempted him to drop out again. But he didn't, and he was able to turn his life around, with the help of teachers who encouraged him to stay in college. He trained as a computer repair and maintenance technician and today he works for the firm that puts together the computers to do the graphics for eighty-five percent of television's weathermen. He trains technicians at television studios, and he's available for major troubleshooting.

His community college experience was so positive that he is thinking about returning to take the math and science he would need to transfer to a university as an engineering major. On a visit back to his community college, he told one of his teachers, "You have to be willing to be educated all your life, in the technical fields especially."

The average student at the community college is an older adult like Patricia, Elaine, or Joe. The average student age is twenty-nine, the largest single age group the nineteen-year-old. But few of even these students attend college full time; only one in five completes a course of study in two years, and fewer than that go on to complete a baccalaureate in just four years. In 1991, only three in ten were attending full-time and of those, the majority were working.

In some respects, Dina Rasor is both typical and atypical. Her pathway is much closer to that of the traditional image of the college student — an uninterrupted four years, two at Foothill Community College, and two at the University of California at Berkeley. But in those first two years at community college, she says she "tried all kinds of different things. I must have changed my major every week. Also, Foothill sent me to Washington, D.C., to work with the National Organization of Women as a summer intern, and that's when I really learned about Washington, and that's when the bug kind of bit me to make sure I would come back." She is now a published writer.

Dina came to a community college quite by "happenstance," as she puts it, and very reluctantly. Her high school grades and test scores had insured her acceptance to a state college in Ohio, when suddenly her parents decided to move, and she arrived in California too late for the UC system application deadline. When real estate people showed the family around they included the community college, where she could enroll in some courses on the first day of classes. Dina's first reaction was "that's low."

For many recent high school graduates, especially those who are well prepared, community colleges are "low," at the very bottom of the collegiate status pecking order. If you have the grades and your family has the money, that's not where you fantasize college life. Or, as one student told us, community colleges "are so ubiquitous, you've seen them all your life, like if you ask a person what color their refrigerator is, they often say white, even if it isn't. It's around them all the time, so they stop seeing it."

John Davidson, like Dina, went straight through two years of a community college and then transferred to a state university. But unlike Dina, he *chose* a community college — Contra Costa in San Pablo, California, because it was "convenient and affordable." He was one of two sons of a widowed, working mother. His high school grades were good enough to earn him a small scholarship for each of his first two years in college, and he could live at home, work in the afternoons and weekends in a local clothing store, and return to the campus library after dinner at home. John went on to get his B.A., and now is national editor of the *Rocky Mountain News*.

Michael W. did not transfer and get a B.A., nor did he leave the community college he attended with an associate degree. Instead, he received a certificate of completion in automotive repair after taking classes for two semesters. He immediately found a satisfying job, and right now doesn't want to think about any more education. But he says he'd return to his community college if he ever went back.

Dina and John were pretty sure that they wanted to transfer, and a recent national poll of students first entering community college indicates that thirty-six percent enter with that objective. Some thirty-four percent say they want job entry skills; sixteen percent, job upgrading; and fifteen percent are enrolling for "personal interest." A "personal interest" student would be one like Patricia, when she first ventured an art class; or Ray, a builder, who takes Spanish courses so that he can do volunteer work in Mexico; or the more-than-middle-aged couple who are enrolled together in a sign language class because the husband is losing his hearing.

But, as we've seen, intentions often change.

ALL OF THESE students were able to make use of open admission and flexible attendance patterns and of the multiple offerings as the need arose. This, we think, is Robert McCabe's point when he says:

> Community colleges can do what no one else can do; we need a lot of help doing it and we need to do it better than we are doing it. But this is the whole issue of dealing with tremendous numbers of Americans, of all ages, who don't have the skills and competencies that are required to survive in this society. That, to me, dealing with that issue, connecting that to programs, not necessarily courses, becomes the center of what we ought to be working on. No one else is going to do it.

McCabe is justifiably proud of the way that Miami-Dade has met the needs of immigrants who have changed the face of Miami.

From the first wave of immigrants, in the mid-1960s, we have been there for every refugee group that has come to this country, this community, from the outside. Fully two-thirds of the professional Cubans in business in Miami have been to Miami-Dade, and this is going to be true of other groups as well.

We help them learn the language, help them learn how to live in this country, help them get the skills to be employed. . . . From the Sixties to the Marriel boat lift [1980], when thousands emigrated from Cuba to Miami, we had some things happen in this community that you wouldn't believe. We had a tremendous number of Cubans living under the Orange Bowl and in tents under the expressway — it was unbelievable.

Miami-Dade's immediate response was to gather staff members who had come from Cuba ten or fifteen years earlier, to produce video material on how to survive in Miami, and to have this staff teaching courses up in the bleachers, as a volunteer effort, to the people who were living beneath the stands.

There have been other waves of immigrants, the latest from Nicaragua. At the college now, more than half the students were born outside of the United States, and English as a Second Language has the largest enrollment of any program college-wide. McCabe says that in the past few years "we have been using almost half of our own privately-raised funds for Nicaraguans because they are here with no services and no way of getting help."

Miami is the city which absorbed the majority of the 700,000 emigrés who left Cuba after the rise of Castro and the thousands who left Haiti, and which continues to absorb other waves of Hispanic immigrants. McCabe feels strongly about these foreign-born students who lack English language skills, and equally strongly about students who may have English skills but lack basics and employment skills. He says, "I think this particular issue — the mismatch between the academic or what I call information skills that people need in this society, and the skills they have, is the greatest threat to the country this side of nuclear holocaust; I think it could destroy us."

Miami-Dade's majority international student population is a reflection of the population of Miami itself, and this mirroring is true of community colleges across the country; "more so than in the universities, the community college student population tends to reflect the ethnic composition of the institution's locale." Minority students constitute 22.5 percent of all community college enrollments nationwide, compared to 17.3 percent in four-year schools.

THE ABILITY TO embrace so many different functions in the same institution is not always easy: it causes periodic debates about *the* proper function of community colleges. Consider:

- They must respond to the demands of the four-year schools to which some students will transfer, but they must not lose their own sense of what it means to provide entry and education to all members of the community.
- They must respond to industry but not give in to it, not turn themselves into narrow training grounds and abdicate their educational mandate.
- They must respond to changing local populations and create for them new gates of entry to American culture.

A program such as Miami-Dade's is unusually comprehensive, but it is not unique. Its role in providing an open door and then fulfilling a broad range of occupational, educational, and ethnic needs is of growing importance to the United States in the coming decades.

Specifics vary from one place to another. What has to be accommodated will vary from one decade to another. Each community has its own set of pressures and demands. But all colleges share a mandate, expressed by a recent commission on the future of community colleges: to "recognize not only the dignity of the individual but also the interests of community" within "a climate in which students are encouraged to collaborate rather than compete" and to include all individuals beyond high school age.

THE VERY COMPREHENSIVENESS of community colleges is under attack these days. But the word "comprehensive" may need some explaining. What it does *not* mean is a supermarket array of courses and programs that students pick at random and with no guidance. What it does mean is that in one place a student can enroll in remedial courses as well as vocational and transfer courses, in a single course for personal enrichment as well as a single course for job upgrade. No one is isolated. England has excellent literacy centers, technical schools, and grammar schools for university-bound students, but they are in different places. In theory it is quite possible to move from one to the other. In practice it doesn't happen all that often.

The comprehensive community college allows and encourages that kind of move. In many ways, it is reminiscent of a huge one-room schoolhouse where students could pick up at any level of development. Quite literally, they see options they might not have imagined. Furthermore, community college counselors help students fresh out of high school who don't know what they are doing or want to do, as well as those returning for whatever the reason.

Mary Day, the Institutional Research Specialist at the Maricopa District in Arizona, told us that "there's a hedge-your-bet sort of thing when [students] come in to the community college. They are adults who are working, who frequently have families and children, and who know that they have to continue working, either to support themselves, their families, or both, so they want to undertake training that will get them immediate jobs, but they don't want to forgo the fact that they will eventually complete baccalaureate or higher degrees. They're essentially hedging their bets. . . . A lot of these people are in the business area — marketing, accounting, computer programming, those sorts of things."

James Edward Oberst (called Jim Ed) "hedged his bets" when he went to Lexington, Kentucky, Community College to seek an associate degree in dental laboratory technology. During his last semester he did an externship at a professional dental laboratory, and during this time decided to continue taking college courses in order to qualify for dental school. When a college is "comprehensive," students can get glimpses into new worlds. When ready to shift direction, they know where to go.

The big question for the turn of the century is whether community colleges will be able to maintain their multiple functions and flexibility. If the colleges begin to impose strict institutional patterns on students—time restraints, curriculum restraints, entrance tests—students will be much less able to find their own way, and chances are, only those with strongly focused goals at entry will feel welcome.

The experience of David's Aunt Minnie points to the dilemma: the pressure for cost-effective efficiency would have pushed her out; the reality of how adults live and make their choices pulled her in. David said that his aunt had been going to her community college for two or three years. She liked being where learning was going on. She wasn't focused. "It was more an environment than anything else. It wasn't to go to college, it was just to be where things were going on."

But then, he says, "her house burned down, she had to move, and she had no idea what she wanted to do. She started doing domestic work for a real estate dealer cleaning houses. Then, still attending classes, she became a cook at a halfway house for men who were just getting out of prison. They liked talking to her, and they came to her with all their problems and she started relaying these problems to their counselors, whom the men wouldn't talk to. One day the director asked, 'Why don't you become a counselor?'"

To become a counselor meant getting an associate degree in psychology. She knew where to go. She went to the community college where she had taken courses off and on for years. She earned the degree. She got the counseling job and went on from there to run the house.

David told us that his Aunt Minnie then started her own program, a halfway house for pregnant women who have a drug problem. It was one of the first of its kind in the nation.

Time magazine described it in a feature article which concluded that "The task is monumental, but [Minnie] Thomas perseveres." Within six years she had founded two more residential facilities and a drop-in center. Apart from her personal achievement and contribution to the community, what is significant is that when ready to pursue more focused study, adults like Minnie Thomas have a place to go that's familiar, where they feel welcome.

"When ready" are key words. Some students may never be. They stay enrolled in a class or two, stay around their campuses "to be where things were going on." Others do "get ready," find their focus, move ahead. In the long run, no one can predict in which group any one person will be.

On the campus of a comprehensive college, students from both groups and from the various areas of study, be it automotive mechanics or psychology, actually see each other, if not in the classroom, at least in the same social area or cafeteria or library or bookstore. Where else except at big sport events do Americans of all ages, classes, races share the same physical space at the same time? Our present ways of living don't provide many such opportunities. Where such exist, we must cherish and nurture them.

Four

Builders of Community, Agents of Change

We propose, therefore, that the theme "Building Communities" become the new rallying point for the community college in America. We define the term "community" not only as a region to be served, but also as a climate to be created.

— The Commission on the Future of Community Colleges, 1988

The public comprehensive community college is committed to serving *all* segments of its community. This task is by no means an easy one, given the changing nature of the various populations served. In California, a state that already has a "minority majority" in its lower schools, Chabot Community College was among the colleges whose ethnic enrollment patterns were not matching those of the graduates of its area high schools. So it hired Felix Galaviz, a member of the local Mexican American community and a Chabot graduate with a master's degree in counseling, to be a counselor, and especially to recruit and work with Mexican American students.

"My job was to go out and talk to them, spend some time on their high school campuses, work with a program that was called the College Motivation Project and get them over to the college. And I did a good job. Several hundred students would enroll. . . . And about three weeks after the quarter got started, they were gone. Fifty percent of them were *pssst!* just gone." Galaviz shrugs his shoulders and waves his hands to

30

indicate his distress. "No matter what I did, I couldn't single-handedly hold them there, and that was very difficult for me."

At the same time that Galaviz was feeling unhappy about the high percentage of Mexican American drop-outs from the college, Chabot English teacher Patricia (Pat) McGrath was unhappy with the way remedial English was being taught at the college. Some ninety students per hour in a lab (with three instructors) were reading units in workbooks and having to pass true-false tests on grammar before they were allowed to write. According to McGrath, it was very obvious that people of color dropped out. So Galaviz and McGrath teamed up "to do something to break the pattern for at least a few students," and Project Puente (*puente* means "bridge") was born.

We were talking to Galaviz and McGrath in an office of the University of California, which had become interested in their project, one measure of their success. Of course, the most important measures of Puente's success were the changes in student learning, reflected in grades, retention, attitude, and the changes Puente affected in Chabot's attitude toward the Mexican American community and the Mexican American community's attitude toward the community college. But we're getting ahead of the story.

Galaviz and McGrath spent six months looking at nearly two thousand student transcripts. "And what emerged was a pattern," says Galaviz. "It kept coming up over and over again: all of these students were avoiding core English classes and other core classes. They would take a few 'safe' courses, such as a little punctuation, library studies, a little pre-math, so they wouldn't fail. And the second thing we found was that there was no coherence, no sequence; no one course followed the other, like 1A and then 1B, and we knew immediately that they just didn't understand the system, how to take courses, the prerequisites.

"One of the things that we discussed over those six months was that some of these kids really did need to talk with other

31

people who had already gone through the system, who had made it academically and made it professionally," says Galaviz. The idea of finding role models, mentors, for the Puente students was incorporated into their pilot project.

All of this transcript reading was done on Galaviz and McGrath's own time since they had no release from other classes or counseling duties. Saturdays and Sundays and an enormous amount of energy went into the pilot project.

For their pilot program, they chose twenty-five Mexican American students who were borderline; they had D averages and "were either on probation or ready to be dismissed from the college." The students were asked to commit to two terms of work, a class below the college English level, and college English composition (commonly called English 1A). McGrath abandoned the skills approach to teaching reading and writing. Galaviz saw the students both in his office and in the classroom. And every student had a mentor with whom he or she had to meet weekly. Many of their writing assignments came out of these student-mentor meetings.

According to Galaviz, who sought them out, the mentors "reflected the community." They were attorneys, real estate agents, judges, scientists, managers in local corporations, computer analysts, math teachers. All were Mexican American/ Latino, and all "very, very busy" people who nevertheless made "a real commitment in terms of time."

Soon the students were no longer "taking courses just to take courses at community college; they were beginning to see the connection between the campus and the completion of these courses," says Galaviz.

The results of that 1981 pilot project were phenomenal. Retention was ninety-six percent. And the students' grades went up; their grade point averages (GPA) doubled. About fifteen percent of this first group subsequently entered a four-year college. "In the core courses they were taking, their GPA went straight up; there was a whole different person," says Galaviz. "They looked different," adds McGrath. "They acted different," Galaviz continues. "This is one of the things

I noticed as a counselor, that they were no longer scared students coming into a new territory; now they were much more involved in the campus, were part of it, felt part of it, and were prepared to work with it. They formed a club; they started to work together, formed small study groups."

Galaviz and McGrath continued their Puente classes for several years, and word of their success got around. A Bank of America Foundation grant allowed them to study the feasibility of replicating their program at other community colleges, and soon a state project was underway, focusing on both retention of Mexican American/Latinos at the community college and transfer of these students to four-year campuses. Galaviz and McGrath now are on grant-funded leaves from their college to assist other community colleges in start-ups. By 1992, Puente programs were in place in twenty-nine California community colleges, with more than thirteen hundred mentors donating sixteen thousand hours a year.

The Chabot program also created a new climate in the community. According to Galaviz, "it changed the attitude of the school administration. The fact that we [the Mexican American community] had so many people out there who were lawyers and judges and scientists — it really changed their attitudes about what was out there and what kinds of resources people had and the kind of professionalism that existed and the willingness to support students wholeheartedly. We had twenty-five mentors at a reception and they all wanted to know 'What can we do to help support the college?' One of the major myths that has been exploded in this program is that the Mexican American community doesn't have any resources to contribute to the students and to the college. They've been giving thousands and thousands of dollars for many years to the students in scholarships. Just this year alone, they gave $26,000 in our little community.

"It also showed how much the Mexican American community was interested in education. The whole attitude — myth — that the Mexican American community didn't care was exploded."

So the Puente project turned out to be a learning experience for more than the students enrolled and the faculty involved; college administrators and Mexican American community members got a new perspective on each other, developed a new respect. The college's relation to its community significantly changed.

It is the constant reassessment of community educational needs that has allowed community colleges to become the largest single sector of higher education in the United States. They have been innovative in reaching out into the community, in inviting non-traditional populations to become a part of educational enterprises.

The City Colleges of Chicago (CCC) is an eight-college system, with campuses spread around the city, but even so students weren't coming to the campuses. Faced with declining enrollment, Dr. Nelvia Brady, chancellor of the system, decided to act. "We were waiting for students to come to us," she says, so they put into effect a recruiting plan that involved going out into the community, with staff attending college fairs, ethnic festivals, and the like.

Then a board member pointed out that many people who were not well educated and who needed skills and training lived in housing projects. So "we literally took the CCC to the CHA [the Chicago Housing Authority] — by bus," says Brady, who grew up in Rockwell Gardens, a CHA development. "From the chancellor to the chairman of the board of trustees, to faculty members — everybody went." They knocked on thousands of doors in fifty public housing developments, telling residents about the programs the colleges offered, explaining how to apply, assisting in the application process.

At the time of this outreach effort, reporters asked Brady how many students she anticipated recruiting by actively making the CCC services known in the community. "I don't care if we only get one student," she replied. "An effort like this sends a message to the community that's much more powerful and far more significant than the number of students you recruit."

Miami-Dade Community College has been quite successful in reaching Miami's burgeoning Hispanic population. But the college admittedly has been less successful with the African American community. One of its most recent college/community collaborations was opening an outreach center in Overtown, the scene of several riots. And the college has moved in other ways to integrate the black community into the college.

"We decided we were going to get one [building] project—we started with one—done by black contractors. The state system in Florida is a nightmare; they make it hard to deal with the bureaucracy. Seriously, from a standpoint of technical knowledge, they make it harder to do the things you have to do to be eligible than to build the buildings," says Robert McCabe, Miami-Dade's president. "So we started by saying the first thing we were going to do is to hire somebody who is an experienced contractor, and that person would then assist whoever got the contract in dealing with the system. The second thing we did was to hold classes for anyone, but especially for black contractors, on essentially how you go about making the bid. You had to take the classes or you couldn't bid the job. And we helped people with the bonding situation as well."

The college got a successful bid from a black contractor. "We also got that person, and one other applicant, in the business of knowing what to do, and since then, they both have gotten several bids on smaller jobs for the college. Part of the idea was to put some people in business for themselves, giving them a lot of help." McCabe and his college board believed "that if you decide the only way you can let a minority contract is to subsidize, and pay tremendously more for it, I don't know if that ever helps them get another job."

Miami-Dade also started a Black Student Opportunity Program, reaching down to tenth-grade black students "who weren't going to be there in the end." They worked out the program with the Miami school system, the school system union, the local chapter of the Urban League, about thirty universities and Miami-Dade's Wolfson Foundation, its fund-raising arm.

McCabe describes the program: "First, the Urban League found a mentor for each student, a successful person, preferably black, who would give time to the student. Second, there was an insistence that the parents or the guardian of that student participate in the program. Third, we worked with the school system on the curriculum. Then we found a sponsor for each student. The sponsors put out around $250 each year. This was matched by the Wolfson Foundation during the tenth, eleventh, and twelfth grade. So the students began to build a scholarship bank account based on grades in the courses we prescribed. When they finished, if they had averaged a B, there'd be enough money to take them through Miami-Dade. Then if they're successful at Miami-Dade, they'll have around $2000 to take with them, and I've made arrangements with thirty universities around the country to take that $2000 and add whatever has to be added so that the students can get bachelor's degrees."

Miami-Dade started the first group of seventy-five tenth graders in the fall of 1987. Of those, seventy-three graduated from high school with B averages, but fewer than half of the cohort came to Miami-Dade; with excellent grades and Miami-Dade's contacts, many were able to enter either a Florida state university, or one of various other four-year colleges; one went to Ivy League Brown. Those who entered Miami-Dade qualified for associate degrees in 1992. While not all the students came to Miami-Dade, Marvell Smith, who supervises the program, considers it an enormous success for all involved—community college, high school, community. And a second group of seventy-five was started through in the fall of 1990.

Miami-Dade was the convener in this complex community group; communications were especially difficult. "It wasn't easy to get the ball rolling," said McCabe, "but I think it's got all the right ingredients. The outside forces have to be there for the student for it to make a difference." The project is not unlike Puente in California, but a financial scholarship ingredient was included. "Having something that looks like a bank book, and knowing you can get all the way through" is essential, McCabe believes. "All you have to do is be successful academically."

The Maricopa Community College District in Phoenix also has acted as a convener of a community group to consider community problems and ways the colleges could work toward their solutions. Nancy Jordan, Assistant to the Chancellor, told us about a project called the Think Tank and how it works. "The high school district in Phoenix and eight elementary school districts participate in it. And we are looking at developing models and prototypes that would have impact on the education of individuals at all levels.

"For example, at a meeting of the Think Tank, the superintendent of one of the elementary school districts said 'If you want to help us, you can work with the parents and these are our needs: literacy and parenting.'"

In responding to these needs, Gateway College (one of Maricopa's ten colleges) had to rethink a parenting program it had developed fifteen years earlier, based on a white, middle-class, two-parent family model. According to Jordan, most of the families that Gateway now serves have single, working parents with limited time. The college's program had to be changed to accommodate family responsibilities, working, and taking classes.

"How do you build a program that maintains a person within the environment that they're in, with all the commitments that they have? If the basic thrust is to make people more effective in the roles they have, then you don't make them sacrifice some of those roles while they're learning how to do it. It seems to me that what you do is to try to accommodate the person at the time," she says.

She believes that parenting has not been considered seriously as a community college curriculum. But "if we are really going to be looking at students as full individuals and work with them, then we should be looking at them as parents, as members of their community, as future leaders."

To be sure, community colleges are not obliged, or equipped, to do what other social agencies should be doing, "which is to handle the social and medical problems of the students that exist outside the classroom, that keep them from succeeding in the classroom," says Myrna Harrison, President of Phoenix College, the oldest and largest in the Maricopa system. But she believes that community colleges should be working with other community agencies, such as state employment offices, health and welfare agencies, even offering them space at their campuses. "Too many agencies have gotten away from what their function is," she says. "If the colleges try to pick up all of those [needed] services, they won't have enough money to do their real mission — to educate students."

Paul Elsner, Chancellor of the Maricopa District, which has 95,000 credit students on ten campuses, inspires his administrators and faculty to see the community colleges as agents of change in the community. When we talked to him in his office in Phoenix, he was greatly concerned about the 250,000 illiterate people in the Phoenix area (about thirty-one percent of the area's population of 788,704), and his fear that a permanent underclass of twenty to thirty percent is "not sustainable." "What we need is a massive structural change [in society] and my feeling is that the community college can be an important social agent to have that happen."

Evan Dobelle, Chancellor and President of City College of San Francisco (a city whose population is largely minority), agrees that community colleges can be, and should be, change agents in the community. "This is the last middle-class white generation that is going to run things," he says. "And what I do every day is try to figure out how I want to be remembered, as the last time my group had a chance to run things. . . . What are we doing about making a transition? This is our last shot at doing something that's going to make an easy transition in a city and a state that is a third world city and state. And that's what's going to happen in America.

"So my attitude for community colleges in the future is absolute partnerships throughout society," he says. "Partnerships with churches of every denomination, partnerships with [school systems], kindergarten through high school, partnerships with corporations, partnerships with nonprofit organizations, partnerships with four-year institutions."

Like Miami-Dade, Maricopa, and City College of San Francisco, many community colleges around the country are involved with high schools and even junior high schools to encourage students to continue their education. In Queens, New York, LaGuardia Community College collaborates with Middle College High School and International High School as part of a partnership between the New York Board of Education and the City University of New York (CUNY). It is one of five such partnerships within New York City.

Middle College High School is for students who have been identified as potential drop-outs or chronic truants. At first housed on the LaGuardia campus, it is now in a building across the street. The curriculum includes internships at such social service agencies as hospitals, libraries, museums, and schools; at the same time, students can fulfill some of their high school course requirements by taking college classes across the street (or elsewhere in the CUNY system). The idea is that becoming exposed to college culture encourages them to live up to the level of college students. The results are dramatic: a graduation rate of eighty-five percent compared to the fifty-six percent officially affirmed for New York City, and a transfer rate of seventy-five percent. Janet Lieberman, the founder of this program, tells us that the high numbers have held steady since the program began in 1974, and that "community support is unbelievably strong." More than thirty-six community colleges throughout the country have created partnerships based on this model; they include Shelby State in Memphis, Tennessee; Los Angeles Southwest; Contra Costa in San Pablo, California; Illinois Central in Peoria; Cuyahoga in Cleveland, Ohio; and El Centro in Dallas, Texas.

An offshoot of Middle College High School in Queens is International High School, designed particularly for students who have been in the United States no more than four years and who score in the lowest quartile on the English proficiency assessment test. A representative cohort can include students from as many as fifty different countries, speaking thirty-six different languages. Teachers speak at least two languages, sometimes three or four. All instruction is in English, with more emphasis than usual on language and on the kind of collaboration that enables students to learn from each other, with the more fluent helping the less fluent. Again, students are encouraged to enroll in LaGuardia classes for some of their course work. This group had been dropping out of the regular high schools in droves; International boasts a ninety-eight percent graduation rate. During one reporting period in 1990, it showed the highest attendance rate in New York City.

WHILE IT MAY sound as though community college administrators spend most of their time being concerned with literacy and other remedial or special programs, that is not the case. Administrators of comprehensive colleges must plan for students whose academic skills cover the widest range. Myrna Harrison describes two afternoon programs at Phoenix College that make the point. First she speaks with pride of Classical Studies, set up for a limited number of students as a "very rigorous first two years of a four-year degree. We're doing four semesters of English," she says, "four semesters of history, four semesters of science. I put Latin in there, and I've been arguing with various faculty about that. It's almost symbolic, for the students as well as the program. To them it means something very special about their academic intensity as well as intention."

Students don't "test into" the program; it's a self-selection process, yet students in the program represent a cross section of the student body at large. They stay together for all their classes for two years; they have lunches together with faculty, go to the theater together, study together. This is called a block program.

But Harrison is quick to add that Phoenix College also offers another block program called Learning Communities, "absolutely the other end of the spectrum from Classical Studies. Students test into it by not having passed any of the tests you take for transfer courses. They test in by bottoming out on the scores." Yet it is organized the same way as Classical Studies: offered in the afternoon when classroom space is plentiful, with committed teachers who work very closely with the students; students stay together for classes, often eat lunch together, do tutoring together. "We are looking a lot more at block programs," says Harrison, "because they keep [students] in and keep them working and get better results."

Paul Elsner says, "The trick is to keep some gaiety to all of this and not make it grim." Making it "less grim" is what many community college programs in the community are all about. Miami-Dade sponsors an annual Paella Festival: Sandra Acebo reports, "different restaurateurs from all over Miami compete to see who can make the best paella — pans are six feet wide — all outdoors, and seven thousand to eight thousand people come to this festival. It involves all sorts of Hispanic culture, dancing, music; it's big, like Mardi Gras, all over the campus. They did it totally on donations for the first three years. Last year they charged twenty-five dollars apiece and the same number of people still came. They put all that money into scholarships for Hispanic students." An annual Book Fair with national speakers draws thousands from around the Miami area. In the year that Miami hosted the 1989 Super Bowl in Joe Robbie Stadium, Miami citizens rated the Paella Festival and Book Fair right up there with the much-hyped sporting event.

Citizens also showed their support in the polling booth when they supported a two-year tax to establish a $108 million endowment for college operations. It was the first tax for the college in its history and it passed just a week after Hurricane Andrew hit the area in September 1992.

Miami-Dade's President McCabe reaped an unexpected personal award for his creative leadership in the community: one of the prestigious MacArthur awards of 1992, which carried with it $365,000 for his personal use. When we talked on the telephone to McCabe about the MacArthur, he downplayed the personal award and talked about the tax issue. "It passed in the devastated South Miami and Homestead areas," he said proudly. He also pointed with pride to the financial backing he is getting from the Miami business community to rebuild the college's Homestead and Kendall (South Miami) campuses and to assist college employees.

Successful community college bond votes give evidence to the symbiotic relationship that exists between the college and the community it serves, say officials. "Our job is to get the message out that the college really serves the community," says Sandra K. Golden, associate vice-president for public affairs and information at Cuyahoga Community College in Cleveland, Ohio, where in June 1992 voters renewed the college's tax levy by a seventy percent margin—a remarkable achievement, "particularly when economic times are tough," Ms. Golden added. In such times, community college tax or bond elections that do not pass may reflect economic conditions and general voter discontent rather than disapproval of a particular college.

OTHER COMMUNITY COLLEGES build community involvement around music, dance, athletics, and drama festivals, art shows, planetarium activities, local history projects, lecture series. Most community colleges make their recreational and other facilities available to community groups on a no-charge or minimum-charge basis. In a number of instances community businesses and other agencies have joined with community colleges to expand or upgrade college facilities. Although corporate gifts are, most usually, in the area of state-of-the-art technology, in Los Altos Hills, California, Hewlett-Packard gave Foothill College $180,000 to create a soccer field and two softball diamonds on the college campus; these are used by the college in the daytime and by corporation employees after work hours.

Kirkwood Community College in Cedar Rapids, Iowa, makes available the services of its video production department to nonprofit community organizations on a direct cost reimbursement basis. Johnson County Community College in Overland Park, Kansas, like many other colleges across the country, publishes a directory of faculty and staff who are available to lecture to local groups. Topics range from services provided by the college to collecting antique furniture.

Central Piedmont Community College in Charlotte, North Carolina, maintains a phone-in information service for the general public called "Dial Our Listening Library." Topics include job opportunities, health care, and local history.

Across the country, community forums have been set up at eight community colleges on a variety of pressing local problems in diverse urban, suburban, and rural settings. The participating colleges are field testing a process to be used by community colleges and citizen leaders in planning, designing, organizing, managing, and following up on these critical issues.

This two-year "test" program has been organized by the League for Innovation in the Community Colleges, with the assistance of a $185,000 grant from the Hitachi Foundation. Issues being explored include "Who took Your Job? Was It Affirmative Action, the Government, or Foreigners?" at Delta College located in the Tri-Cities Area of Michigan (Saginaw, Bay City, and Midland), where General Motors and related businesses have either shut down, cut back, or moved to new locations. Lane Community College in Portland, Oregon, has also explored a topic related to jobs: "Striving for Unity: Economic Transition Programs for Workers and Communities in the Timber Crisis." Kirkwood Community College in Cedar Rapids, Iowa, has established a forum on young criminal offenders, "Adjudicated Youth and the Service Delivery System."

Many community colleges offer classes at senior centers throughout their service areas, or hold programs attractive to seniors on campus during afternoon hours when the morning crush of students is over and the students who come after work have not yet arrived.

In California, Monterey Peninsula College has for seventeen years offered a team-taught program called GEN-TRAIN, "the history, politics, literature, drama, art and philosophy of Western Civilization in fifteen two-week classes." GENTRAIN, which stands for General Education Train of Courses, is not exclusively for seniors, but its afternoon hours and flexible entry/exit times makes it a class of "mostly white-haired folks," according to one participant.

Other colleges offer open entry, open exit courses, or offer over a period of two semesters what normally would be offered in one: a foreign language with heavy lab requirements, for example, which normally might meet seven hours a week for one term would be scheduled for three and one-half hours a week for two terms. Low-impact aerobics is popular with seniors, and at one community college a seventy-five-year-old woman placed high in women's weight lifting. We know of a one-hundred-year-old woman who finally received her associate degree; the home for seniors where she resided threw her a party.

Many older students, however, elect to take the morning classes, which normally attract younger students, on the college campus. A retired engineer of our acquaintance signed up for one poetry class and ended up earning enough credits to transfer as an English major to the university where he had originally earned his engineering degree. When he died recently, he left money for scholarships at the community college.

Ironically, *Modern Maturity*, a slick, four-color bi-monthly magazine of the thirty-two million American Association of Retired Persons, published as its August–September 1991 cover story an eight-page article about older people going back to school, but devoted only one sentence to community colleges. Admitting that "money remains the most serious problem facing older students contemplating a return to school," the article then stated: "Less expensive options include continuing-education courses and community colleges, which offer a wide range of associate degrees and certificate programs."

We don't want to be unfair to the AARP. The Association, in cooperation with the League for Innovation in Community Colleges, did help fund a survey of community college programs for older adults. However, the results are published in a thirty-six-page publication, which will be read by few except community college administrators; *Modern Maturity* (free to members) is number one in circulation in the United States.

THOUSANDS OF NON-CREDIT courses are offered by community colleges each year, with students usually bearing the cost of instruction. Courses range from Chinese Cooking and Basic Obedience Training for Dogs to Introduction to Personal Computers; however, the majority of classes are continuing education courses to upgrade business and professional skills. The American Association of Community Colleges estimates that five million Americans are enrolled in community college non-credit courses or activities each year.

Frequently it is these non-credit courses that become the focus of community college critics who complain or joke about a "Mickey Mouse" curriculum. When a midwestern state voted in 1988 to allow pari-mutuel betting on horse races, a community college in that state offered a course in figuring handicaps. This was reported on an evening network news program, but the course never was identified as non-credit and paid for by the enrollees, not by taxpayers. Though this may have made a funny endpiece, it really isn't.

The newest area of how community colleges relate to the community (affecting the community, being affected by it) is in a variety of alliances with business and industry. Such alliances are not limited to community colleges, especially when firms are national. For instance, some sixty community colleges and four-year colleges are now involved with IBM in a project called the CIM [Computer Integrated Manufacturing] in Higher Education Alliance. One of the community colleges involved in the alliance, DeAnza College in California, received more than $300,000 in IBM computer hardware and software. The grant assures IBM of a CIM demonstration laboratory, and IBM will own and maintain the equipment for three years, after which it will belong to the college.

The college/local business-industry alliances grow out of the vocational mission of community colleges, out of their need to keep abreast of technological advances and to have the latest in hi-tech equipment available for their students, and their need to find qualified instructors in certain areas. All over the country community colleges employ part-time instructors with special abilities, and many of these instructors are full-time workers in high-tech industries.

The alliances also grow out of the needs of community businesses for both technical and academic in-service courses for their employees, as well as for students with associate degrees and training in the latest technology — be it manufacturing or health related. But here, again, an ongoing tension: the danger of such alliances is that industrial training may get confused with education, that the potential of the students is sacrificed to the relatively narrow needs of an industry.

Many community colleges work with populations in prisons. Many have large enrollments of students who watch lectures and demonstrations on TV, stay in touch with their teachers via telephone, mail in assignments. Maricopa Community College District in Phoenix has been a leader in incorporating community concerns such as homelessness, environmental needs, health, and the like with academic study, encouraging students to volunteer with community agencies. Back in 1978, E. L. Harlacher and J. F. Gollattschek recommended that the mission of the community college should include being "a vital participant in the total renewal process of the community ... dedicated to the continual growth and development of its citizens and its social institutions."

More recently, the Commission on the Future of Community Colleges, sponsored by the American Association of Community and Junior Colleges, urged the colleges to become community education centers responding to local needs: "The community college, at its best, can be a center for problem solving in adult illiteracy or the education of the disabled. It can be a center for leadership training, too. It can also be the place where education and business leaders meet to talk about the problems of displaced workers. It can bring together agencies to strengthen services for minorities, working women, single parent heads of households, and unwed teenage parents. It can coordinate efforts to provide day care, transportation and financial aid. The community college can take the lead in long-range planning for community development. And it can serve as the focal point for improving the quality of life in the inner city."

Five

Teaching Today's Students

There are community colleges, where thousands of able and intelligent men and women take their teaching opportunities with the greatest of seriousness and give more than value received. These institutions, with ties to their parent communities, free for the most part of the snobbish pursuit of the latest academic fads that so warp their university counterparts, and free also of the unremitting pressure to publish or perish, are, I believe, the hope of higher education in America. Unheralded and scorned or patronized by "the big boys," they carry out their mission with spirit and elan.

— Page Smith, *Killing the Spirit*

*T*he primary responsibility of any community college faculty is teaching, and community college teachers are in an ongoing struggle to find more and better ways to let students integrate what they bring from their lives with what their classrooms have to offer. The faculty who are most effective are aware of the interrupted patterns that describe the educational lives of so many of their students: David or Connie (who speak in Chapter 3), Pat or Joe (whom we describe in Chapter 4), the evening student who works all day and takes classes two, three, or four times a week, the reentry single mother who misses class when her child is ill, the laid-off factory worker who returns to retrain — they are very different from the mythical junior college students of "the good old days." As the myth goes, such students were young high school graduates with few responsibilities outside their school work.

Becoming aware of interrupted patterns, accepting them, learning to connect with the different waves of students they work with—all this leads back to teaching and learning. It leads into the classroom. Julie Maia, who speaks later in this chapter, recalled how her "instructors made attempts to make whatever you're reading or studying or looking at, connect to people's lives as they're *really living*" [our italics].

What this means is that community college faculty who are effective, who like where they are and what they are doing, are often compelled to learn to teach in ways for which their own professional training provided few models. Indeed, teaching at a comprehensive community college forces the often uncomfortable recognition that what higher education in America is really about is teaching, learning, and working with people who are not like us, *whoever* the "us" might be.

THE NEXT YEARS will see many new teachers. In 1986, 110,909 full-time and 164,080 part-time faculty members were teaching at community colleges, with some forty percent scheduled to retire within this decade. Unquestionably, the new teachers of the coming decade will affect the atmosphere, perhaps even the direction of many community colleges. Where do they come from?

Vocational faculty come from jobs in the field—nurses, welders, electronic engineers. Some faculty come from teaching in high schools. Most liberal arts faculty come from graduate schools that still teach little about how students learn, certainly not adults from various racial, ethnic, or cultural backgrounds. Community college faculty may face underprepared students; often they also begin as underprepared teachers.

Solid training in the discipline, or experience in the professional field, and the inclination to teach are obvious prerequisites. But there seem to be others, less obvious.

All lower division college programs offer introductory courses, but for community college faculty that word "introductory" takes on new, literal, often double-edged meaning. Take Helon Raines, for instance, a native Mississippian and mother of two children, who began teaching at Casper College in Wyoming, straight from graduate school in creative writing at the University of Denver. She was hired to teach in the Coal Field Tech program, to "bring a humanities and writing component to men who would ultimately go out and be heavy equipment operators in coal mines in Gillette and Rock Springs and other places."

Both she and her students were being introduced to new worlds. Her students were electricians and welders and many of them had no serious interest in academic studies, she recalls, "but many of them were very curious about the sort of things we did, just reading short stories stimulated, opened up worlds." And their instructor? She too was being "introduced" to new worlds.

"Some of the best students I ever had at Casper College or anywhere were among these men," she now thinks, and then adds, "Teaching at a community college is a very humbling experience. It means that you have to be a generalist, you have to be very versatile, you have to be very adaptable. I think the first thing it did was bash any elitist ideas I had cultivated at the University."

Now, thirteen years later, Helon Raines teaches the whole range of writing courses, has served as chair of her department and participates in many national conferences. In these years, she says that she also has learned to teach in new ways, no longer "standing up in front of the classroom talking to them," the model she herself had experienced as an undergraduate student and graduate student. "The conversation, I like to think, instead of beginning with me, begins with the student."

This willingness to introduce ever-changing student populations to a discipline or skill and be introduced by them to new challenges is a requirement for vocational faculty as much as for liberal arts faculty. Phil Wall, who teaches welding, came to teaching after many years in industry, which is not unusual for faculty hired to teach vocational classes. The interviewing process would eliminate applicants without sufficient experience in the field they want to teach in. Most of his students are "between the ages of eighteen and thirty-five." He describes "working with the young and trying to stay one step ahead of them" as "a tremendous challenge and joy."

Some eight hundred hours of training are required to get a person from knowing nothing about welding to entry-level welding, ready to take a structural steel certification test. Phil teaches future professional welders; he also teaches people who want to learn "just enough to fix their own car, do their own work," and he teaches art students who use welding for sculpture.

"The two areas that I really enjoy the most," he says, "are [teaching] the basics to students who are just coming into the program, who have never had any welding at all, and watching them grow. Tremendously rewarding. And the other one is forcing those art students to pick up enough of the basics so that they can get creative. When you get into the advanced students just trying to hone their skills, I can turn that over to one of the night instructors and let them do that." For Phil Wall, the work with students least like him—beginners and artists—presents him with the challenges he enjoys most.

COMMUNITY COLLEGES SEE hundreds—thousands—from new groups of students, and they will continue to do so. Men in Coal Field Tech, beginning welders, boat people from Vietnam, middle-aged women making their first attempt to enter the paid working world, Latin American refugees, the list mirrors our population. Some are academically competent, some not, but many come from backgrounds altogether outside American academic culture.

For Evan Dobelle, Chancellor at San Francisco City College, "counseling in a community college is almost as important as teaching." He thinks "the biggest problem we have at this institution is self-esteem, not cognitive ability. Once you get people believing in themselves, most of these people do well, even in cases where they have problems in basic skills."

Counselors are part of the faculty. Counselors like Felix Galaviz (in Chapter 4) are involved in a large variety of functions and can make a huge difference in the life of students. They help plan class schedules; they test for placement, advise students on course and program requirements, suggest sources for additional help they might need. They do career counseling (often with the help of interest and ability tests); they do personal counseling; they are the experts on which of the community college courses are accepted by each four-year school.

Many students see a counselor only when they need a signature for a course schedule or a specific bit of information, like a prerequisite for a given class. But for many others, a counselor can become advisor, coach, friend, and a personal link on a large campus. Often it is the men and women who teach and counsel at comprehensive community colleges who shepherd many of their students across cultural boundaries, who help them bridge class divides. In order to do that, and in the process of making it happen, many of the most successful faculty discover within themselves the source of the teacher-student learning bond.

Consider Carmen Rezendes, one of many community college instructors who began teaching at a community college with no intention of staying more than a few years. She interrupted a Ph.D. program because, she told us, "I was tired of graduate school and I was going to take a year off. What I loved when I started was the teaching. I mean, I just loved teaching. There was something spectacular about the intimacy of teaching, especially after graduate school.

"There had been something so impersonal in so many of my graduate classes, and I felt closer to my students in the community college. Any place I've ever been in a classroom, I've always felt somewhat naive, but it always seemed to me that the game, the academic game, was to hide your naivete and try to pretend you knew what was being talked about.

"One of the things that really refreshed me was that people [community college students] hadn't learned that academic game yet. Their naivete shone through and it inspired a kind of enthusiasm in them. Or maybe the enthusiasm was allowed to flow rather than being stifled by 'let's pretend we all know what's being talked about. How do you spell that name he just mentioned that I never heard of before that everybody seems to know?'"

She is able to empathize with students who not only do not fit into conventional academia, but perhaps do not fit into traditional American culture, who are immigrants and frequently the first in their families to attend college. "My parents came over, so I'm a first generation American." When she teaches a course she particularly loves, so-called "bonehead" English, "I feel as if I am paying back to ancestors in a way. It's like I feel as if I am teaching *all* of my relatives, that they're getting off the boat and I am helping them across the gangplank in terms of the bridge. I feel that there's a kind of empathy that I have for this situation because they're moving from one culture to another in becoming academically literate, in the sense of being able to do college writing."

Nancy Jordan of Maricopa district in Arizona speaks in a similar vein. "Because I was born in Mexico, I never really fit in anywhere, and I always felt like a dislocated person; still do to some extent. But I think that all of this gives me a special feel for how people feel when they come into systems that are really large and you don't know how they operate, because I've had to do that over and over in my life."

Capacity to empathize and to adapt can come from many, many places. It can come from having had a good experience at a community college. A recent study reports that approximately forty-four percent of community college faculty have attended community colleges as students. Paul De Bolt, a very personable young man who heads a one-person journalism department and coaches girls' basketball at Contra Costa Community College in San Pablo, California, is a good example of such instructors; he had been a student there before transferring to San Diego State University for his B.A. and M.A.

"I never wanted to go to Contra Costa, because it was a junior college. It wasn't so much my parents pointing me away from it as it was the peer thing. I got into the University of California and spent a year at Berkeley. But I didn't like it over there. The atmosphere, I think, just wasn't right for me.

"I was thick-skulled; they were trying to tell me what was best for me, philosophically, the type of education I should receive if I wanted to be a newspaper reporter, and I didn't agree with them, so I came over here. [Contra Costa College is nine miles north of the Berkeley campus.] And I just fell in love with this place," Paul said. "It was a people place . . . just the way people interacted. I just couldn't believe it." His journalism teacher was Alma Oberst, a professional newspaperwoman who herself had zigged and zagged through higher education, returning to school in her early forties to finish a B.A. in English and earn an M.A. in Journalism.

"She sort of took me under her wing, and I was able to write for a student newspaper, get things published. I played basketball and I was editor-in-chief of the paper. It was a wonderful experience. It changed my life, coming to Contra Costa." Among other things he counts as a benefit is meeting his wife. Eventually, he was hired to replace Alma Oberst when she retired.

"I love teaching here. It's incredibly satisfying to work with students who, for some reason or other, have ended up at a community college. . . . They need a second chance academically, they are underprivileged financially, they want to be retrained, to enter a new job market, they may even have emotional or physical ailments." Like himself in his student days, he says, they are looking for a special environment.

The capacity to empathize with, adapt to and learn from one's students is not an intellectual ability. Often it grows on the job. Often it surprises, with the sudden recognition of "I like it here. I like the students, I like the work, I like the atmosphere."

Susan Forman teaches math at Bronx Community College in New York. She had intended to be a high school math teacher, but like Carmen Rezendes, she landed at a community college almost by accident. "I liked the students a lot," she told us, "and what was interesting, I grew up in an upper-middle-class community on Long Island, where as far as my mother was concerned, everybody who wasn't Jewish was Italian. That's her perception of the world. There're the Jewish people, the Italian people, and the other people and she's not sure who they are.

"I had never, until I was teaching at Bronx Community College, seen a black child. Ever. I had never seen a roach before I moved to New York City. My parents aren't well-to-do, but certainly [they live in] a totally different environment than anything that my students knew, [but] in fact I got along extremely well with my students—I really enjoyed them; they certainly seemed to enjoy my classes. And I just stayed on and on."

Eventually she wound up with a Ph. D. in Math Education, doing all her course work at night. After she finished her dissertation she started doing some math-anxiety work, and "as time went by," she says, "what I found, much to my astonishment, was that my female students saw me as a role model, which was a shock, because to me—the gap is enormous. The women in my class felt that if I could do it, then they could do it." Susan now thinks that this "was a real turning point for me, professionally. It made me feel a lot more responsible for what went on."

IN ACCORD WITH the root meaning of the word education (*educere*: to draw out, to lead forth), men and women like Helon Raines and Phil Wall, Carmen Rezendes and Nancy Jordan, Paul De Bolt, Susan Forman, and thousands of their colleagues learn to see themselves more as educational guides or coaches, less as high judges or stern gatekeepers to the inner sanctum of a given discipline.

This is not to say that community college students are passed through Chemistry 1A, for example, because the course is a watered-down version of what is taught at a university. Community college instructors are aware that their students may transfer, may become science majors, and their course outlines, texts, and lab assignments match those at a university. Generally speaking, the intent of instructors is not to weed out students, but to find ways to help as many as possible master the material. Instructors are tied more to the learning of the student who may need a boost here, a nudge there, less to the discipline and the department.

Which does not mean that the teaching faculty at a community college is not interested in theoretical developments in their fields. Quite the contrary. Some twenty-five percent of the non-occupational faculty and ten percent of the occupational faculty have doctoral degrees, although the master's degree is the usual academic requirement for teaching. A majority of faculty, both full- and part-time, belong to national professional associations, and a significant number participate at national and regional conventions and meetings. But in community colleges, this commitment to one's own discipline or department leads primarily back into the classroom, rather than to research and publication.

"Clarity of commitment to teaching is an important element in the job satisfaction displayed by community college faculty members," says a 1990 Carnegie Foundation report on community colleges. It also recognizes that "this same commitment to teaching can and does lead to a reduced involvement in research." Faculty members for whom research, scholarship, and publication are the most valued career activities will most likely be unhappy on a two-year college campus. They can feel cheated when faced with teaching situations they did not anticipate.

But by far the majority of community college teachers are happy with their commitment to teaching and with their institutions. When the Carnegie Foundation asked two-year faculty members "How do you feel about your institution?" sixty-five percent rated it "a very good place for me," while only forty-one percent at four-year colleges replied as positively.

Another bit of evidence comes from a 1984–85 study that set out to test the conventional wisdom that the higher the educational level, the better, the more satisfying and fulfilling the professional life. The study surveyed three hundred full-time teachers from fifteen institutions in Los Angeles county, five secondary schools, five community colleges and five four-year institutions, and asked each to complete a Faculty Satisfaction/Dissatisfaction Scale measuring ten areas of job satisfaction.

All three levels of faculty reported general satisfaction with their jobs, but community college faculty ranked highest. The authors of the study found that community college faculty "prize their association with their students and colleagues." They concluded that "perhaps these teachers have found the community colleges to be the right 'fit' in meeting their personal and professional needs. The community college offers a setting where the faculty may justifiably feel that they have a teaching career worthy in its own right, not a stepping stone to a 'higher' level of education." That personal connection, it seems, is a chief source of satisfaction among community college faculty.

WHAT THEN ARE the complaints? For full-time faculty, the list is headed by heavy teaching loads and large classes. One math instructor we know teaches a calculus class with forty students; his son's calculus class at a large state university is much larger, over one hundred and fifty students in a lecture hall, but it also has discussion sections of fifteen run by teaching assistants and the university lecturer teaches two courses per term, not five.

For part-time faculty, the list is headed by their part-time status, which carries with it poor salary, few benefits, minimal job security, little recognition, and perhaps no office space or pay for holding office hours for students, preparing for classes, or reading papers or exams. Often there is too little opportunity to know their colleagues.

The dilemma of part-time faculty is a major issue. For one thing, their sheer numbers create problems. Around sixty percent of faculty at community colleges are part-timers, some teaching only one class, some up to fifty percent of a full-time instructor's load (for much less than fifty percent of the full-timer's pay). It is estimated that about twenty-five percent of all community college credits are earned through classes taught by part-time instructors.

There are two groups of part-time faculty. A good many are specialists with full-time employment outside the college, often in high-tech firms; they bring a diversity and breadth of experience that enrich classroom teaching. They are experts in a particular computer language required for government contracts, oceanographers who teach a course in a physical science division that cannot support a full-time oceanography department, published authors who teach one course in creative writing. Many are gifted teachers. They teach because they love teaching and want to be a part of what the community college is doing in the community, rather than because they need a job.

But there is another, larger group of part-time faculty who very much want full-time status. Many of these, too, are gifted teachers, but they *do* need the job. For them, it often feels like simple exploitation (although interestingly enough, they too express a high rate of satisfaction with their work). Colleges keep them as part-timers for financial reasons: they cost less per hour than full-time faculty and they are more easily let go when money is short and there is a reduction in the number of classes being offered. Many of these men and women teach at several different colleges in order to make a livable income. Some eventually get hired into a full-time position; some have to give up and take a job in a non-teaching field.

One of the problems with having so many part-time teachers is that frequently they are not fully integrated into the college community. They may not have time to advise students; they may not be around in the daytime (may not be invited or compensated) to work with colleagues on curriculum, academic standards, or other discipline-oriented issues; they may not be hired in the same way as full-time faculty and they may not be as carefully evaluated or mentored.

It should be said that community colleges are not the only postsecondary institutions using part-time faculty. Universities employ their graduate students to teach many of the lower division sections and small classes, and often have lecturers who are not on the tenure track and get hired from year to year. Four-year colleges, too, gain scheduling flexibility and save money by employing part-timers when and where needed.

Wherever it happens, it's exploitative. But there is little hope, in this time of tight budgets, that colleges will begin to shift many part-time positions into full-time appointments.

Nationally, part-timers constitute the majority of the faculty and their ratio is rising. At the very least, as the Commission on the Future of Community Colleges points out, "for community colleges to fulfill their potential, part-time faculty, regardless of their numbers, must be carefully integrated into the institution. For these colleagues, the need for orientation and professional development is even greater."

JULIE MAIA IS one of the new instructors, who began full-time teaching in 1990, one month after her fortieth birthday. She has also herself lived the zigzag pattern. She can speak with experience as a community college student and a university student, as a four-year college instructor (where she taught part-time) and a community college instructor.

Julie never expected to go to college. She grew up in Salt Lake City, which she describes as "a very conservative community, and I figured I would get married and have children and that was it. I didn't think that I'd have a career." She now also thinks that her father, who worked for the Army repairing machinery, found it threatening to have his children more educated than he was. He had been an immigrant from Slovakia, and "*his* big accomplishment in life was graduating from high school."

Julie followed the script she grew up with. She graduated from high school, moved to California, got married. By the time her marriage fell apart she had a child of her own and was raising a younger half sister. "At that time," she says, "it felt like my life fell apart too. I felt very trapped. But I was always a reader, so when my son entered kindergarten and my younger sister was in first grade, I had four hours a day to myself and I knew I wanted to do something with it. What seemed the most available was to go to some classes in college and see where I could go with that."

And so her own formal higher education began when she was twenty-eight years old, a single mother of a five-year-old, and on welfare. Now, twelve years later, she says, "I want to be a teacher who actually makes a difference in someone's life. I want to teach in a community college. I want to teach people like me, or like the people I was tutoring."

But that isn't whom she's teaching. Although her college is only forty miles from the college she herself attended, her students are unlike any she has ever faced or known. She describes them as seventeen- or eighteen-year-olds, many of whom come from conservative, fundamentalist families, mainly white. Her greatest initial challenge, she told us, were the students who believe they're in college only because their parents want them to be there (either get a job or go to school), not because *they* want to be there. "For me," she said, "every minute was important."

But at the end of her first semester at this new job, having just finished reading sixty bluebooks, she also told us, "I have the best job in the world. These were a thrill to read. Some who never understood that reading is exciting, got it. They began to sense why they were in college. They are changing."

What she emphasized most strongly to us was that teaching or being taught in a community college to her means that it's "personal, which means in some way that it's constructive for people who have lives outside the classroom." The question "What does this mean to me?" — or put differently, "How do *I* understand this?"—was encouraged and heavily weighted. Put still differently, she was explicitly encouraged to integrate what she brought with what the classroom had to offer. To connect. To draw her own mental map. For her, "the real door opening was the door of the world of ideas." But, she is quick to add, "Ideas and life as it's lived go together; they're not separate."

She describes studying Freud's "Civilization and Its Discontents" in an introductory philosophy course at community college: "We did of course talk about it within the history of ideas, but we talked more about what Freud has to say. We tried to bring up examples, personal examples from our own lives to clarify his ideas, so that when he starts talking about how he doesn't understand the oceanic feeling, we would talk in the classroom about different experiences of the connectedness of religious feeling and that sort of discussion doesn't go on too much at the university, I think."

Her philosophy course at the university she describes as a "huge lecture course, a man was sitting up there talking about philosophical theories and I wasn't thinking as hard. I was taking notes. I was learning what he had to offer, but I wasn't thinking out the problems myself. I wasn't evaluating for myself whether Machiavelli's theories about a state actually make sense. And in the smaller more intimate classroom, that's what you get to do."

But not always. Linda B's experience as a student was frustrating. She had always believed the Bible story of creation as unquestioningly as her anthropology instructor believed the theory of evolution. Many Lindas now attend all campuses. But at the time, when creationism was smilingly dismissed by her community college instructor, Linda was enraged.

Given the clash of such fundamental world views, perhaps nothing could have satisfied Linda or, initially at least, made her less angry. What seems significant, however, is that she didn't know how to talk about her anger or her dismay or her confusion, and moreover felt she had no one to talk about it *to*. She tried to deal with it in a vague and unfocused essay; then she dropped the class and almost, she said, dropped school. Her instructor never knew.

Like Linda, many academic newcomers will feel isolated and alienated, up against it, if they can find no linkage between the social dynamics of their lives and the academic values that are taken for granted in the classroom. As Julie Maia said, "Ideas and life as it's lived go together; they're not separate."

BECAUSE COMMUNITY COLLEGES are deliberately inclusive, their faculties are required to learn and relearn to work with people who come from many different backgrounds. Often this means that teachers need to profess less, to create new and better ways to listen to and understand what students bring.

Powerful advocates for academic newcomers, often under-prepared newcomers, are Glynda Hull and Mike Rose, who have written extensively on the frequent mismatch between what a teacher expects and what students do. For Hull and Rose, "the desire for efficiency and coverage [of a set body of material] can cut short numerous possibilities for students to explore issues, articulate concerns, formulate and revise problems." They argue that "the real stuff of belonging to an academic community is dynamic involvement in generating and questioning knowledge, that students desperately need immersion and encouragement to involve themselves in such activity, and that underprepared students are capable—given the right conditions—of engaging in such activity." This becomes "knowledge-making" rather than simply knowledge receiving.

Community college classrooms are the sites of much pioneering work in "knowledge-making." Smokey Wilson's basic reading classroom is one such site. She teaches students whom people like David and Julie help tutor. These are students who don't read or write or do math well enough to enter any of the programs the college offers. The problem is past achievement, not ability. Her classroom could be seen as a permanent laboratory designed to discover how students learn.

To begin work on vocabulary, for example, she and her students develop lists of words that are new to the students. Mitch, a local heavyweight boxing champion whose sweater is bordered by a three-inch black mink collar, selects "flamboyant." He likes the way it sounds and looks. "It describes me," he says. "I'm cool. I'm flamboyant."

The next week, the class reads a passage written by Malcolm X and talks about what he means by "a stock of knowledge." Soon afterward, Mitch tells the instructor she has her "game down." She's not sure what having her game down means. "It means," he tells her, "you've got your stock of knowledge together."

Mitch is connecting school language to life-outside-school language; more than that, he and his instructor are learning to translate to and for each other. Both are attempting to build and cross bridges between their worlds and the world of academe, to connect without leaving behind their own cultures. This is a very different process from the staple of many basic English classes and vocabulary texts: Learn ten new words a week, use each in a sentence, prepare for a ten-minute quiz every Monday; spelling counts.

The Puente Project (Chapter 4) is another example of how individual faculty struggle to create better learning situations for their students. Pat McGrath and Felix Galaviz recognized a group of students who were failing — unnecessarily, they felt. They tried to figure out what didn't work and what would work better. What they created has become a successful statewide program. Puente has trained teachers and counselors who have replicated the program in twenty-nine colleges. California Mexican American/Latino students now transfer to four-year schools in numbers unheard of ten years ago.

What is discouraging is that too often, pioneering and successful methods and techniques are still part of "special" programs or "special" classes, not part of regular teacher education or of regular student experience. There are very few mechanisms to tie formal research to classroom reality, to integrate classroom findings into graduate school education.

So far, individual instructors who want a better understanding of how educational theory ties to classroom practice, a better understanding of how students learn and why students fail, must rely on their own initiative, time, and energy. They find conferences, summer programs, additional course work. Few formal links exist.

One of the few attempts to link practice and research is sponsored by Patricia Cross, a community college expert, recently on the faculty at Harvard, now at the University of California, Berkeley. Her most recent project linking research and practice (co-authored with Thomas Angelo) focuses on what she calls classroom research, a process in which "classroom teachers can, through close observation, the collection of feedback on student learning, and the design of experiments, learn more about how students learn, and more specifically, how students respond to particular teaching approaches."

A key assumption is that "the research most likely to improve teaching and learning is that conducted by teachers on questions they themselves have formulated in response to problems or issues in their own teaching."

What is cheering is the unusually large and spontaneous response to *Classroom Assessment Techniques: A Handbook for Faculty* that describes thirty such classroom research studies, their purposes, possible uses, pros and cons. Unadvertised, and with no promotion, the booklet sold ten thousand copies, with an estimated eight thousand to community college faculty. Community college faculty, it seems, are keenly aware of the need to learn more and better how to invite students in and up.

We talked with Pat Cross in her comfortable faculty office, which overlooks live oak trees and the Berkeley Chancellor's residence. She sees the 1990's as the Decade of Faculty. "Ultimately," she told us, "if we are going to improve learning, it's the faculty who are going to do it."

This is very much what Robert McCabe of Miami-Dade told us when he said that "the next major focus in community colleges has got to be on what happens inside the classroom—to really make a significant improvement there.

As far as I'm concerned, that's where the focus in going to be for the next ten years."

Community college faculty will always have to deal with new kinds of students, reach beyond the teaching strategies they began with. This has been true for at least thirty years. It promises to be even truer in the coming years.

Much will now depend on the new generation entering community college teaching. They will need to understand that many of their students are zigzagging their way through higher education, and they will need the support of their colleagues, their colleges, their communities, and their professions.

Six

Initiating the Uninitiated: The Uses of Language

The hard part is not in identifying winners; it is in making *winners out of ordinary people. And that, after all, is the overriding purpose of education. Yet, in most periods of educational reform in the past, education has reverted to selecting winners rather than creating them.*

— K. Patricia Cross, 1984.

Literacy is contagious. You catch it from a teacher.

— Smokey Wilson, 1994.

*M*any students who have done well academically come to community colleges. They come because the campuses are close to home, because tuition is relatively inexpensive, because four-year colleges are limiting enrollments. They take courses and move on — to degrees, to certificates, to work. They are accustomed to success.

But community colleges also serve students who haven't done well. Millions of adults regret that they sat in classrooms but turned away from schooling during adolescence; they later return, hoping to pick up where they left off, to catch up, make up for their previous lapses.

And there are millions more who never had the chance at all. They are not in need of a latter-day remedy; they need a first time opportunity to learn what schooling teaches. This group includes the thousands of kids who are now growing up homeless, the thousands who drop out of school early on, and the thousands of immigrants who were not educated in their first language, much less in English.

None of this is new. In the 1970s, Mina Shaughnessy, who directed the Instructional Resource Center at the City University of New York at the time of that institution's shift to open admissions, divided entering students into three groups:

- Those who met the traditional requirements for college work.
- Those who had survived their secondary schooling but not thrived on it.
- Those who had been left so far behind the others in their formal education that they appeared to have little chance of catching up.

Four-year college teachers knew the first group best, were familiar with the second group, but were totally at a loss with the third. Here, Shaughnessy tells us, were

> the true outsiders ... strangers in academia, unacquainted with the rules and rituals of college life, unprepared for the sorts of tasks their teachers were about to assign them. Most of them had grown up in one of New York's ethnic or racial enclaves. Many had spoken other languages or dialects at home and never successfully reconciled the worlds of home and school, a fact which by now had worked its way deep into their feelings about school and about themselves as students.
>
> They were in college now for one reason: that their lives might be better than their parents', that the lives of their children might be better than theirs so far had been. Just how college was to accomplish these changes was not at all clear, but the faith that education was the one available route to change empowered large numbers of students who had already endured twelve years of compulsory schooling to *choose* to go to college when the doors of City University suddenly swung open.

Most four-year schools have since closed those open doors; community colleges are the primary institutions left in higher education that deliberately invite all three groups. They

continue to see their task as initiating the uninitiated —
whether it be into academic literacy or collegiate student-
hood, or into the workplace and new or better jobs: the intent
is to open doors to new skills, new disciplines, new and more
complex ideas at all levels.

These initiations begin inevitably with classroom language.
Entering college students find themselves surrounded not
only by new words but by a kind of talk that identifies who
is inside and who is outside of academic culture.

The impact of new vocabularies is the most obvious. New
words, the ability to talk like a lawyer or a cosmetologist, mark
everyone's entry into new fields and worlds. The secret pass-
words become shared. And used. As those words become familiar and accepted, the new entrant begins to feel familiar and
included and achieves a kind of solidarity with the new group.

This is true of the neuro-surgeon, the plant pathologist, or
the economics major who initially had no idea how to distinguish macro-economics from micro-economics. It is equally
true for the new immigrant whose mastery of clichéd idiom
is the first step of belonging. A relative, newly arrived in New
York, would proudly repeat on all summer occasions, "It's
not the heat, it's the humidity."

Immigrants are all too familiar with how language connects
to a sense of belonging. But immigrants also know the loss and
disorientation they feel when they find themselves in that no-
man's land between cultures. In that respect, their experience
is not unlike that of Mina Shaughnessy's strangers in academe.

In her book *Lost in Translation*, Eva Hoffman puts it poi-
gnantly. She remembers how, as a Polish teenager newly
arrived in Vancouver, new words, new expressions picked up
from school exercises, from conversations, or from books had
no associations, did not give off the radiating haze of conno-
tation, did not evoke. "It is the loss of a living connection,"
she writes.

Students who have done little reading and less writing know
all about that loss of a living connection. The inexperienced
writer, the "basic writing student," may feel particularly

discomfited. Not only are there new words and new expressions (one student had the courage to ask, "What is an S. A.?" after an essay assignment), but familiar words suddenly take on strange meaning. Writing no longer means handwriting; reading no longer means deciphering words.

Many community college teachers work with students who have little experience with what is meant by "main idea" or "theme"; students who, even if they know how to write a lab report, often do not know what it is supposed to do or what it's good for. Or why a research paper should be more than a stringing together of secondary sources. Or what we mean by evidence. For these students, strangers to most aspects of college, every classroom seems to be full of land mines.

But in this chapter we are talking about more than learning new vocabularies to negotiate in new worlds, or learning to write for different audiences. We mean something richer and more pervasive: we mean initiation to and practice with a kind of talk (and writing) that characterizes academic or collegiate culture. We are talking about inviting students to do what Mike Rose calls "entering the conversation." How can we do that?

One illustration comes from Margot Dashiell's ethnic literature class in a basic skills program at Laney College. She knows that her students have distinctive taste in music, in clothing style, what have you; but she also knows that printed words and writing have always been flat for them, without life, not worth having a taste. Her goal is to demonstrate that it's worth it.

One thing we know is that taste comes with experience. So Dashiell begins with a poem like Langston Hughes' "A Poet Speaks of Rivers." The poem is read aloud, students can read and hear at the same time, and she asks students to pay attention to what appeals first, a phrase, an image that jumps out. Students then call these out "like at a Quaker meeting," she says. "'Ancient, dusky rivers', 'My soul has grown deep like rivers', 'I bathed in the Euphrates' — just a pile of phrases, but each one with a beauty. We'll talk a little bit about why this or that particular phrase was so appealing, so we're talking *about* it. Then I begin talking with them about metaphor and simile, that this is the language that poets use, that it's something that occurs in literature all the time. We'll pick out similes and metaphors in songs and poems and talk about what the metaphor and simile does. 'My heart is in chains' —what have you got? And then we go back to Langston Hughes' poems ['The Poet Speaks of Rivers,' 'Mother to Son'], and see that they're really a series of metaphors."

Dashiell is leading her students across a great divide. She provides experience, evokes and accepts all personal responses and leads to the kind of classroom language that we like to call analysis. Equally important, she hopes that "by first getting a real feeling for what is on the page"—in this case a poem, "students will learn always to speak out of their conviction. If they don't like it, they'll know why. And if they like it, they'll know why."

The four-year college or university can assume, perhaps justifiably, that their students enter knowing how to participate in their education or, at the very least, can find out how. Community colleges assume no such thing, and especially in pre-collegiate classes, they are much more apt to start with where the student is.

The Puente Project (Chapter 4) provides another telling illustration. Most of the students (all Mexican American newcomers to academic culture) initially avoided all English classes, which seemed to be of little use except as an invitation to failure. McGrath and Galaviz turned that perception upside down. They combined English instruction—reading, writing, talking, listening—with an intense mentor and counseling program and made new uses of language real to the student.

Mary K. Healy, who was Research and Training Director for Puente before becoming Director of the English Credential Program at UC Berkeley, told us that students "find it very easy to write about their mentors. The mentors are real, they're right there, they talk to them, they can write down the quotes, and they have an absolutely avid audience back in the classroom because the other students want to to know about their mentors. And so they're writing for very real audiences."

Puente is designed as a language-based program in order to "increase the number of Mexican American/Latino community college students transferring to four-year colleges and universities"; forty percent of their students do indeed transfer, but significantly, only four percent of that group then major in "communications." The uses of language are the means, not necessarily the end.

Language helps socialize students into the use of rhetorical strategies required for school, into knowing in a practiced way the difference between opinion and analysis, for example, and how these get used in academic culture. The Puente model is a particularly winning example here because in it students are not asked to give up an old culture in order to enter a new one; success in academic or Anglo culture need not mean betrayal of Mexican American culture, though it may mean negotiating conflicts between competing styles of home and school. The program succeeded with an initial group of students who had D averages and who "were either on probation or ready to be dropped from school."

The Puente model introduces students to college dialogue by writing, talking, writing again, talking again, reading. "Who's doing the talking has seemed to me the crucial question," says Mary K. Healy. "I'm getting to the point now where I say to our Puente teachers that in any class the students should have a couple of chances to write, several different opportunities to talk, and probably their talking will be done best in a small group that is fairly well structured so that students know that they are purposeful and have some reason for being in the group.

It's ironic that we accept this view of learning for graduate seminars, but seem to forget all about it when it comes to entry level classes. Healy notes how frequently it's the traditional picture of the teacher talking and the students sitting there fairly passively.

Talking, of course, has a political dimension. As she points out, "Who's talking at that particular moment has the power in a situation. The only situation I can think of that is not empowering when you talk is when you're reciting in response to a question some teacher has asked you. But surely students come into a sense of their own power to the degree that they're listened to seriously by the teacher and by other people in the class."

To risk ideas and responses in words, to be taken seriously and not be made to feel foolish: that's how strangers to academe learn to feel comfortable in their new environs. Often they need the connection to at least one committed tutor or teacher, one other person who is willing to draw the less-tutored student into the new talk, and thus the new culture (a process that holds well beyond specialized programs like the above).

Mike Rose describes how this works, how in his first semester in college he felt out of his league, drifting through required courses, "simultaneously feeling contempt for and exclusion from a social life that seemed to work with the mystery and enclosure of the clockwork in a music box. . . . I went to school," he says, "and sat in class and memorized more than understood and whistled past the academic grave-yard. I vacillated between the false potency of scorn and feelings of ineptitude."

What happened to Rose is that his high school teacher intervened, and the chairman of the English Department, Dr. Carothers, volunteered to look out for "Art Mitz, Mark Dever, and me . . . and agreed to some special studies courses that we could substitute for a few of the more traditional requirements, courses that would enable us to read and write a lot under close supervision of a faculty member. In fact, what he promised were tutorials."

There follows a touching description of teachers who sat with him and talked through his work as he was "struggling to express increasingly complex ideas, and . . . couldn't get the language straight," coming up with sentences like this: "Some of these modern-day Ramses are inherent of their wealth, others are self-made."

His instructors stuck with him. Rose reports that "he'd grumble" but finally this "linguistic parenting felt just right: a modeling of grace until it all slowly, slowly began to work itself into the way I shaped language."

Inherent in the success of bridge programs and courses, and central to Rose's description of linguistic parenting are the strong but not always explicit connections among language, learning, and human interaction. Here are adult applications of ideas first addressed by the Russian linguist Vygotsky in 1936. In describing the relationship between language and learning in young children, he was looking at that "zone," as he called it, "that exists between what people can recognize or comprehend when present before them, and what they can generate on their own"—that zone where "what the tutor *did* was what the child could *not* do." To use an adult example, it is that space (or should we say time?) where we can follow the tutor/teacher as she explains and solves a problem or assignment; we might even be able to work it out ourselves with appropriate prompting, but faced with a similar problem or assignment and left to our own devices, we are at a loss. As the instruction or tutoring proceeds, however, learners take over parts of the task that they were not able to do at first but that, with mastery, they now become consciously able to do.

Jerome Bruner puts this in a slightly different way, saying that the learner "must 'borrow' the knowledge and consciousness of the tutor to enter a language." It is what a colleague of ours, Smokey Wilson, calls "catching literacy." In incomplete learning, we borrow and parade language and consciousness without ever making it our own. We talk about superego, ego, and id. In genuine learning, we begin to own the new language and knowledge, which means we can use it in wonderfully new ways never thought of by our original tutors.

David Mullen (Chapters 1 and 2) describes how this can work. He was tutoring a young African American student, a single parent who, he said, "had no real interest, or thought she had no real interest." She had been given an open reading assignment, and he suggested Toni Morrison's *Sula*. They then talked about the story, its characters, and what it all might mean. She read some other books by Toni Morrison, and they talked about them too. "From then on," David said, "she was committed to reading—she talks about books, she talks about actual story structure and how things happen and why things happen and that's something new for her. It gave her a different way of looking at her own life, putting her life in perspective."

This kind of experience demonstrates, once again, the difference between education and training. Education is a process that slowly leads the students into some *engagement* with the subject or task, and that process almost inevitably relies on language: the tutor/teacher explains what needs to be done, shows how it's done and guides through practice—here is Rose's "modeling by grace." Training, on the other hand, says here is the right way of doing it, and relies almost exclusively on skill and drill and memorization. Thus one can train students how to set up the experiment, but not how to interpret the results. One can train students how to answer comprehension questions, but not how to get personal meaning from reading. The above examples demonstrate, finally, how students who enter the conversation "become increasingly adept at seeing the same set of events from multiple perspectives." An anthill, say, can be looked at from the perspective of a sociologist or of a botanist. Columbus' voyage can be seen from the perspective of a fifteenth-century Spaniard or of an American Indian.

Becoming increasingly adept at seeing the same set of events from multiple perspectives depends at least in part on the uses of language. Given the deepening of ethnic, racial, and cultural hostilities worldwide, it may be the most significant survival "skill" for all of us. It has always been central to education, and is perhaps the single most important skill for the academic outsider who is looking for entry into academic culture. But it is also becoming an important qualification for almost all segments of the American workforce. A recent study on vocational education for health care professionals reports that "employers were generally satisfied with the technical skills training that new employees had received in secondary and postsecondary vocational education programs" but dissatisfied with "the communications, leadership, and decision-making skills of entry-level employees.

"In every occupation studied, employees had assumed greater responsibility for explaining complex procedures to patients, were working with patients who were older or had language difficulties, and were required to produce more complex written documentation.

"The researchers recommended increasing the focus of instruction on communications, leadership, and decision-making skills through the implementation of integrated vocational and academic programs."

Our own experiences confirm this. Respiratory or radiation technicians, for instance, need to do more than measure lung capacity or set high-tech machines. They need to be sensitive to the patient who is anxious or in pain, know how to explain what the patient must do, what the dials mean, how the machine works. The technician whose explanation reassures patients has a dramatically different effect than the technically competent technician who is inarticulate or cold.

IN THE CLOSING paragraphs of her book, *Errors and Expectations*, Mina Shaughnessy worries that many of the programs for underprepared students "have been stretched more tautly than is necessary between the need to make haste and the need to teach the ABCs of writing in adult ways." She worries "how many students of talent have left our programs not for want of ability but for the sense they had of being done in by shortcuts and misperceptions of educational efficiency."

She concludes with a question still in process: "Just how we are finally going to reconcile the entitlements and capacities of these new students with our traditional ways of doing things in higher education is still not clear. As we move closer to this goal, however, we will be improving the quality of college education for all students and moving deeper into the realizations of a democracy."

Shaughnessy's pioneering work gave legitimacy to open admission programs in all institutions of higher education: to welcome and teach all groups of students, not only those who already feel safe and familiar with academic culture; to look more closely at how students learn and find better ways of teaching all students. It will improve, she predicted, not dilute college education for all.

Throughout our book, we concern ourselves with what will happen as more and more well-prepared students come to community colleges. As much as we welcome their entry, we worry that the door will get narrower and the threshold higher for others. The community college stands as the only torchbearer left for Mina Shaughnessy's vision. At City University, the opening doors were beginning to close even before Shaughnessy's untimely death in 1979.

Janet Emig, a colleague of Shaughnessy who was teaching at Rutgers University at the time, wrote that "Mina lived long enough to watch at CUNY, her university, what many of us are watching at our own — the quite systematic dismantlement of what she had so laboriously built, to which she may have quite literally given her life. She was even asked to participate in the demise and destruction; for the Savage Seventies are nothing if not thorough in trying to divest us of our most hard-won beliefs and actions.

"There is, I believe, only one adequate and appropriate memorial to Mina: that we enact her courage; that we find the current retreat — no, rout — into the elitist irresponsibility of earlier decades, where once again we agree to teach only those who can learn without our active and imaginative efforts . . . Mina truly believed, without sentiment, in the republic as the shining city on the hill. And she would undoubtedly agree with many of us that unless, as a community, we reverse ourselves and the direction that our schools, colleges, and universities are currently taking, this country is truly no longer morally habitable."

Granted, community colleges, their staffs, and their students are far from perfect. Poor teaching, disaffected students, bureaucratic snarls exist, as they do elsewhere. But community colleges are attuned to stand behind, not in front of the student, to be sponsors more than gatekeepers, to generate the talk and interactions within the classroom that bring the academic outsider into the collegiate culture.

Seven

Educating a Vital Workforce

The substitution of knowledge for manual effort as the productive resource in work is the greatest change in the history of work, which is, of course, a process as old as man himself. . . . Education has moved from having been an ornament, if not a luxury, to becoming the central economic resource of technological society.

— Peter Drucker, 1977

When we first started writing this chapter, a friend said, "You can't write about today's economy; it's a moving target." That the economy is a "moving target" is just our point. The facts are that employment needs have changed and will continue to change, millions of unemployed and poorly employed Americans need more and different work skills, and community colleges are institutions that have a long history of training and educating workers and facilitating their transition from school to workplace.

More recently, community colleges also have been facilitating the transition from workplace to classroom, as work requirements change, or jobs disappear. Community colleges offer the academic skills which new jobs require — from basic reading, writing, and math to entry-level computer competencies and interpersonal skills. The line between training and education is blurring. In our reading we often found the terms used interchangeably.

What makes community colleges fit so neatly into the "moving target" economic picture is that while analysts predict that by the year 2000 only one out of four workers (the

professionals: scientists, lawyers, doctors) will require a baccalaureate or higher degree, they also say that "entry to three
out of four jobs will require some form of postsecondary education."

"In recent years, the really good companies in the United
States have reorganized the workplace to take workers
beyond their muscle competence," according to William
Brock, chairman of a 1991 Labor Secretary's Commission on
Achieving Necessary Skills (SCANS). While only five percent of U. S. companies have so far reorganized into "high
performance workplaces," many experts feel that this is just
the tip of the iceberg. U. S. companies will need to reorganize, and U. S. workers will need to retrain in order to survive global competition. In fact, unskilled work is being automated or exported out of the U. S. job market. In its report,
the SCANS commission indicated that "more than half of our
young people leave [high] school without the knowledge or
foundation required to find and hold a good job."

When we talked to Paul Elsner, Chancellor of the Maricopa
Community College District in the Phoenix area of Arizona,
he described his visit to an automotive plant in the Detroit
area to illustrate how non-competitive the high school graduate has become. "They have extraordinarily automated
plants. The old industrial plants were dirty and noisy and
[the new plants] are still kind of dirty and noisy, but they are
tied to computers. So the plant is run by design engineers and
technicians. They have not hired a high school graduate in
eight years from any of the high schools in that area."

Chances are good that many of the computer technicians
hired at the robotized auto plant are community college graduates. More than seven out of ten technicians—such as medical technicians, computer programmers, air traffic controllers,
and paralegals—in the workplace today do not have baccalaureate degrees, but gained their employment skills by enrolling
in formal occupational education programs or on-the-job
courses from employers. Sensitized to local job market needs
through business and industry advisory councils, community

college occupational programs routinely upgrade the technology and course content to provide their graduates with the best chance at a job.

There is a misconception that technological change eliminates jobs; rather it redistributes them to industries demanding stronger basic skills. Nor does technology "deskill" or "dumb down" jobs; technological jobs require greater skills. "Mass production techniques during the first half of the twentieth century led to the 'dumbing down' of many craft jobs by reducing them to simple, repetitive functions. But robotics, microprocessors, and the revolution in telecommunications have abruptly reversed this trend," says economist Roger J. Vaughan.

In addition to technological change, the demand for education and occupational skills is being influenced by two other factors. The expansion of trade has increased the demand for skilled labor relative to the demand for unskilled labor. Most of the jobs lost over the past two decades have been semi-skilled and unskilled jobs in manufacturing. More of the jobs gained through the growth of exports require relatively high levels of "human capital"—high wage manufacturing, transportation, and transactional activities, which include finance.

A second influence is that most new jobs are created by new businesses, few of which offer their own training programs, and most of which need employees who can perform several roles. There are eighteen million businesses in the United States today, and the Small Business Administration estimates that by the year 2000, that number could increase to twenty-five million.

The point is that perhaps never before in their half century or so of existence have the community colleges of America been so well positioned to play a major role in America's future. If we as a nation decide that "high skills" is our route to the future, there is no better institution than the community college system to address the massive education effort this will require.

There are various ways in which citizens can use their community college to enter or change their working life. One way is to *choose from a community-job oriented roster of career programs leading to a certificate or a community college associate degree.* Occupational fields include accounting, administration of justice, agriculture, air conditioning technology, animal health technology, automotive technology, biotechnology, business (including small business management), carpentry and construction, computer programming, computer integrated manufacturing, cosmetology, day care, dental assisting and dental hygiene, electronics and engineering, environmental technology, fire science, food science, hotel/motel management, landscape technology, legal assisting, library technology, machine tool technology, nursing, office automation, ophthalmic dispensing, pharmacy technology, radiation therapy technology and other health-oriented programs, sheet metal, telecommunications, travel and tourism, welding. Some community colleges offer one hundred or more different occupational programs; job needs in the local community determine which programs are offered at the individual colleges, and program enrollments ebb and flow depending on the local job markets.

These programs attract both poorly educated and highly educated students, students lacking in confidence and students lacking in specific job skills. The poorly educated — students who are weak in reading or writing or math — often take a remedial course in one of these subjects or they may take a whole program of basic skills to prepare them for admission to the vocational program they have chosen. We say more about that later in this chapter.

Coming from the other direction, graduates of four-year or two-year colleges with liberal arts education but no currently marketable job skills can enroll in one or more courses or a sequence of courses leading to associate degrees or certificates in career fields. This kind of reverse transfer is being made more difficult in some states, notably California, by increasing tuitions and fees for those students who already hold degrees.

Elaine Dormshield was this kind of student; she graduated from a prestigious university without job skills and a number of years later when she needed to go to work, she enrolled in a community college health program. So was Frank M., an engineer with both community college and four-year college degrees, who, at age forty, re-enrolled in the community college in order to take a short sequence of courses leading to a certificate in supervisory management.

The actual educational choices and pathways of students in vocational programs undermine some of the conventional wisdom that surrounds occupational or vocational education, namely, that these programs are "terminal," narrow-gauge tracks for the academically less able students who have neither the intention nor the ability to go on, and that low income and minority students are sidetracked onto these programs and so kept from moving onward and upward.

Reality can dispel our conventional wisdoms, and a close look at actual student records demonstrates this. Clifford Adelman directed one of the very few longitudinal studies that examined postsecondary transcripts for over twelve thousand students over fourteen years. One example he cites, presumably not atypical, are the courses taken by a student who earned an associate degree in engineering technology:

Microbiology	Marriage and Family
Games and Exercises	Psychology of Adjustment
Calculus I	Principles of Economics
History of the U.S.	Social Problems
Texas Government	Architectural Drawing
Engineering Drawing	Organic Chemistry
Principles of Accounting	Introductory Sociology
Introduction to Business	Business Communications
Calculus II	Basic Technical Drawing

Neither Adelman nor we see anything terminal or narrow-gauge in this course of study. Classifications need to reflect what students do, their actual choices, not what they say they will do or what researchers extrapolate from limited evidence. Otherwise inferences, assumptions, and policies get built on sand.

And what has been happening, to the surprise of the educational establishment, is that an increasing number of community college students are successfully transferring from vocational programs to four-year colleges — say from a secretarial science program to a business major, from occupational therapy into health fields requiring a baccalaureate. Their pattern often is zigzag: from community college to job, back to community college for four-year collegiate prerequisites, to college or university.

According to Alison Bernstein, who was the program specialist charged with community college affairs at the Ford Foundation when we interviewed her, community college vocational or career students may outnumber so-called liberal arts transfer students in actually transferring.

We talked with James Palmer, until recently Director of Data and Policy Analysis for the American Association of Community and Junior Colleges, about this phenomenon. In a recent study he found that twenty-six percent of the students who were in occupational classes or programs said they intended to transfer. He told us that "the old myth is that vocational education is where the less able students are cooled out, but this trend belies that notion."

He also found that "low income students enroll in high status and low status program areas in almost equal numbers; and highly self-confident students equally tend to enroll in low status program areas, just as students with below-average self ratings of ability are as likely to enroll in high status programs." (The skill levels of many jobs change and increase, and what is low status today child care worker, diesel mechanic may not be tomorrow, in pay or status in the community.) Students write their own scripts more often than not, despite stereotyped expectations.

Yet the community college vocational curriculum too often still is viewed in hierarchical terms — ranked above remedial but less academically demanding than programs that transfer to a four-year college. This map no longer fits the territory, at least not on this level. Even the classifications are dubious and seem to exist mainly for funding and bureaucratic purposes. But once internalized, old maps are hard to redraw.

Fred Mitchell at Madison Area Technical College in Wisconsin talked to us of the "stigma" that vocational education has on it. "People on the street don't understand that whatever it is they're doing is a vocation, anything that helps them get there is vocational, going through high school is, going to college is, particularly if you want to be a lawyer or doctor. They still think *vocational* is a dirty word."

He himself went to a technical college and became a welder. After the service, he married, had a family, and went back to college. When we spoke with him, he was Assistant Director of Instructional Services. In Wisconsin, the seventeen two-year schools are called technical schools, and only three are permitted by state law to offer college parallel courses. One of these is Madison Area Technical College, which has six campuses and serves more than sixty thousand students a year. Their ages, Mitchell told us, "vary from sixteen to sixty-six or seventy, which is also kind of nice, which is what we should be about. The average age is probably around twenty-nine."

"I believe in what we're trying to do," he said. "Because I know, I *know* that people can go through here and go out and get a job and begin to earn and produce. . . . I think they learn something in a community college or technical college (I use those synonymously) that they don't lose, that is the realization that Yes, they can learn. Yes, learning is a kind of a lifelong process. Yes, it will not end when I walk out of this door, but in the meantime I know when I walk out of this door I'll be able to earn some money. If I want to go back, for whatever reason, I can, and I know that they won't look down upon me because I did come back, because when I was there I saw a lot of people who did come back, so I feel more comfortable doing it."

Remember Connie in Chapter 2. "Coming back" describes the second half of her pathway, when she wanted to upgrade from being a licensed vocational nurse to becoming a registered nurse. She managed to find a community college program that allowed credit for her LVN study and experience (which means that she saved a year because she did not have to go back to square one). But admission to that transitional program required completed course work in anatomy and physiology, and in microbiology. Connie "came back" to the community college she knew best, re-enrolled and successfully completed these two courses while she was still working as an LVN. (Both courses, incidentally, are classified as collegiate transfer courses.) She then "came back" (in a different way) to another community college which was offering the special RN program that she could complete in a year's time.

COMMUNITY COLLEGES STAY in touch with the economic and social realities of their communities in a number of ways. One of the most common is the use of advisory committees formed before new programs are initiated, and kept in place throughout the life of the program. These committees advise on curriculum, facilities and equipment, the nature and extent of employment needs, and they establish criteria to evaluate the performances of students completing the requirements for any given program.

Frequently, as we've noted before, businesses donate equipment or lend facilities furnished with state-of-the-art equipment. This can be medical equipment, as local hospitals act as training centers for students enrolled in community college programs for registered nurses, radiation therapists, respiratory therapists, emergency medical technicians, and other medical specialists. It can be specialized computer equipment provided by space engineering firms. In Kansas, Johnson County Community College and Burlington Northern Railroad joined to build an Industrial Technical Center on the JCCC campus to provide classrooms and technical facilities, including a locomotive simulator, for both institutions. Three

A. S. degrees are offered and many certificates. Some thirteen thousand students have been through the center since it opened in 1988. In Arizona and Illinois, where Motorola has plants, the company has extensive relationships with community colleges.

Sometimes programs are designed to retrain entire factories, if necessary. St. Louis Community College, for example, contracted with the Ford Motor Company in St. Louis to retrain their workforce while the company was robotizing its plant; six months later, all the Ford workers had been retrained, kept on the payroll, and were working in a brand new plant.

Company retraining, however, has been more the exception than the rule. When Patricia Anne Revis' sewing plant in Marion, North Carolina, closed, that was it. There was no large-scale retraining program, and she lost the sewing job she had held since age sixteen. But she was motivated to enroll in Western Piedmont Community College. "My dream has always been to go to college," says Patricia. "I wanted to be a nurse. But I was getting older, and it seemed harder to examine my dream." Then in 1988, the company president "read a short statement that brought my dull, unexciting little world down around my ears."

Patricia is "retraining" for a totally different kind of job, one with many present and predicted job opportunities: she is in a vocational program leading to an associate degree in nursing. "At work I used to feel that my body was moving faster than my brain. Now my hand can't keep up with what my brain wants to put on paper."

NEW PARTNERSHIPS AMONG community, college, and business and industry are increasing. One illustration is Rock Valley College in Illinois, which now has an $8.7 million Technology Center, financed by local taxpayers who approved the sale of revenue bonds to build it. Leaders of sixty local businesses are helping to plan training and technical exchanges. According to Dr. Karl J. Jacobs, president of Rock Valley, "The idea is to create more jobs, more employees and therefore more people in the community who will pay more taxes, and that benefits everyone, including us." Jacobs sees the college's growing ties with local manufacturers as a matter of "bottom-line self-interest."

It is this bottom-line self-interest that troubles people like Alison Bernstein. "Not," she told us, "that there is anything wrong in doing business with business and industry. I think it more has to do with the fact that in general, industry is interested in its own bottom line, and educators are interested in student development."

In the *New York Times* article that describes the Rock Valley Technology Center, Bernstein is quoted as saying, "Community colleges are functioning more and more like training institutions for local employers. They should not sell the shop to the employer without worrying about the educational needs of their students. They must make sure their students have enough English and history and social science, the concrete skills for job mobility." It may sound strange to hear English, history and social science referred to as concrete skills for job mobility, but these are the new realities.

The report put out by the Labor Secretary's Commission on Achieving Necessary Skills (SCANS) identifies five competencies and a three-part foundation of skills and personal qualities "that are needed for a solid job performance." Competencies are listed as:

- *Resources* — allocating time, money, materials, space, and staff.
- *Interpersonal Skills* — working on teams, teaching others, serving customers, leading, negotiating, and working well with people from culturally diverse backgrounds.
- *Information* — acquiring and evaluating data, organizing and maintaining files, interpreting and communicating, and using computers to process information.
- *Systems* — understanding social, organizational, and technological systems, monitoring and correcting performance, and designing or improving systems.

- *Technology* — selecting equipment and tools, applying technology to specific tasks, and maintaining and troubleshooting technologies.

The "Foundation" required for competence is:

- *Basic Skills* — reading, writing, arithmetic and mathematics, speaking and listening.
- *Thinking Skills* — thinking creatively, solving problems, seeing things in the mind's eye, knowing how to learn, and reasoning.
- *Personal Qualities* — individual responsibility, self-esteem, sociability, self-management, and integrity.

There is general consensus that today workers need to possess an intellectual framework to which new knowledge can be added. This kind of intellectual framework grows when learners on every level are offered access to ideas and not simply drilled in tasks: when they are led through mathematical experiences that require more than memorization; when they explore the meaning of what they read or do or design; when they are encouraged to write.

Writing Across the Curriculum programs, for example, which exist in many community colleges, ask students to respond in writing — whether it be to ideas, to designs, to processes, and whatever the particular course of study. The student in ornamental horticulture cannot just draft a garden design; he must write about it, "see it with the mind's eye" and describe it, defend its advantages. The student in algebra cannot just solve the problem; she must explain her steps to another student in writing; she must play the teacher in a teamwork situation. This kind of writing is more than learning course material in the process of thinking and writing about it; it mirrors the ideal world of work described by the SCANS report.

WHAT ALL THIS leads to is the big question of training *versus* education, and what role community colleges should play in preparing students for work.

The difference used to be seen in terms of subject matter. In the nineteenth century, the young gentleman who was studying Latin and Greek was being educated, whereas the blacksmith's apprentice was being trained. Activities of the mind were seen more as education, hands-on activities more as training. But the study of Greek and Latin often consisted of gruelling exercises in memorization, referred to as the training of the mind. Rote learning, it seems to us, is almost always training. Education demands discussion, reading, writing, thinking; it asks for analysis and judgment. Training prepares people for fixed situations, for a narrow set of tasks. McDonald's trains its employees to work at the counter, to push appropriate pictures of food items on cash register keys. Education, on the other hand, prepares people to analyze and understand a variety of situations, or, put differently, to adapt their know-how to a variety of situations.

Vocational education, then, is very different from vocational training. Fred Mitchell, a strong supporter of vocational education, says that an industry which does "training very narrowly for a specific job" doesn't educate a person "enough so that he or she can go across the street if they opt to, or move their family, and go to work in another place."

Alison Bernstein thinks along similar lines. She cited as an example Xerox University in Leesburg, Virginia, a residential facility for 1,500 Xerox employee students. Most of them come to learn how to repair Xerox equipment, and they can learn that in four to eight weeks. (Xerox is third in money spent on job training, following IBM and General Electric.) "They can train people in that facility with computer-assisted instruction—the most high-tech stuff you've ever seen—to fix, as this guy put it, eighty percent of what goes on with a Xerox machine. And they can do it fast, they can do it in a way that's highly efficient, sort of state-of-the-art instructional stuff."

The problem with this, Bernstein says, is that "when you get to the next twenty percent over just mastering what this training module taught you, you're into something that isn't training. You're into something called education. And that's something that business doesn't want to pay for, because it's a whole lot harder to measure the results of that. And I guess what I'm saying is that to the degree that business will work with community colleges to educate [up] to the eighty percent, one has to be careful that you're not simply doing for business the training that is the minimal requirement rather than the education which takes it beyond that eighty percent.

"I'm not prepared to say that the business of the community college is over if it does the Xerox University part, because the Xerox University part leaves out what I'm calling the education. And the reason why Xerox University is entitled to leave it out is because they're not interested in the education of students. They're interested in better employees. And there's a difference between better qualified employees and an individual's educational advancement."

Some colleges and business/industry groups seem to be finding middle ground. In our own area of California, which includes Silicon Valley, home of semi-conductor and computer manufacturing, local employers nearly tripled—to $4.4 million—the amount they spent on contracting community college instructional programs from 1988 to 1990.

Contract instruction works something like this: the local community college sends instructors to local companies and charges the company for each course offered, regardless of the number of students enrolled. The charge to the company covers the instructor's salary plus extra pay for travel time, some percentage for administrative overhead, the cost for classroom equipment and supplies, and sometimes the cost for students' texts. However the contract is figured, its intent is to keep the financial burden with the company and off the taxpayer.

If the college develops a special curriculum for the company, all college costs, including faculty hours, are paid for by the company. When a college teacher and a company official work together on course outlines, the company benefits from the educational expertise, and the college develops an up-to-date curriculum it can use in its own classrooms. Frequently the companies donate state-of-the-art equipment to the college.

Employees of some businesses get released time to enroll and earn college credit for their studies; frequently they continue to take community college classes and earn enough credits to be awarded certificates or associate degrees. Some contract instruction, however, is non-credit.

Some ninety-four percent of public community colleges offer at least one course on a contract basis to public or private employers. Most frequently offered are courses that deal with job-specific skills, followed by courses in basic reading, writing, and math. Much of this training focuses on helping businesses adopt new manufacturing or office technologies. Community colleges also have contracted with the federal government to retrain technologically displaced workers and other displaced workers; one such program is the Job Training Partnership Act.

Here are two contract programs described in the morning newspaper: DeAnza College, situated in the middle of Silicon Valley, "sends instructors to local companies such as Amdahl, Apple, GTE, Hewlett-Packard and IBM, where it educates and trains more than 3000 workers a year with courses in such areas as industrial management, accounting, business administration, quality management and English as a Second Language."

Or, "When Advanced Micro Devices decided last year to close an aging semiconductor manufacturing plant . . . , the company found that most of the employees there lacked the skills necessary to work at its new state-of-the-art factory. Rather than fire the employees — who had been with the company an average of 10 years each — AMD signed a contract with Santa Clara's Mission College to re-educate and re-train workers who might otherwise lose their jobs. Each of the 70 employees chosen to participate is spending 28 weeks full-time in class at company expense studying math, chemistry, physics, English and communication skills."

But how about the students whose basic academic skills are too low to qualify for Xerox University, those who are not "chosen to participate" in the AMD: Mission College retraining program, or those who fail the English as a Second Language course offered at their factory?

Employers spend thirty to forty million dollars a year on training, something like 1.2 to 1.8 percent of annual corporate personnel expenditures. According to the American Society for Training and Development, 49.5 million workers needed, but did not receive, retraining in 1989, and a third of those needed basic skills education. A minimum of corporate training and education budgets are devoted to basic skills education.

Most community colleges, however, offer basic skills courses and programs designed to prepare students to enter or re-enter the workforce. They welcome students with or without high school diplomas, including those at the bottom of the occupational ladder who are often the most invisible.

The success of one young man illustrates the need. Donald was on worker's compensation when he first enrolled in a community college; a back injury on the job made it seem very unlikely that he would be able to return to his factory occupation. His worker's compensation counselor saw him as borderline, with limited capacity for retraining.

But at Laney College he enrolled in a special program that offered much more than rote skill training, a "bridge" program designed for students with low literacy and math skills, and with no college experience. At the same time, he helped deliver audio-visual materials to classrooms on a work-study program, and found a mentor and friend in his supervisor.

He thrived. After two semesters in the program he was able to write a six-page research paper called "A Worker's Look Into The Glass Container Industry." This is his last paragraph: "I was the youngest of six children. I've worked in the glass industry for 11 years. Since I worked in the factory, the only writing I did was filling out time cards and signing my check. Coming back to school has been more rewarding than anything I have ever dreamed of."

His instructors and his work supervisor met with his workers' compensation counselor, showed her his work, and she was able to see him in a new light. He was placed in a training program for copy machine repairs, which he successfully completed and then advanced in the company to his own repair territory.

The story illustrates an important point: employers train their best-educated employees. "Employers cannot fill the skills gap," confirms economist Roger J. Vaughan. "Basic skills and occupational skills are complementary: employers hire and train those employees with the best education, training, and experience. Employers cannot do what David Kearns, chairman of Xerox, calls 'the product recall work for the public educational system.'"

Without community college basic skills education, this young man would have had little chance to be trained by an employer. As things now stand, in ten years or so he may be back at the community college to take supervisory management or other courses that will help him move up in his job, to get an education beyond what the copy machine training program provided. He may. There are no guarantees.

REMEDIATION AND BASIC skills are relative terms. They carry little meaning outside specific contexts. Basic skills for a culinary arts program, for example, might mean fractions; for a radiation technician program, it might mean intermediate algebra. "Functionally illiterate" used to describe people who were unable to write their own names. Today it describes students who test below the tenth-grade level.

Accurate numbers are hard to come by, but even if one subtracts by a third, it is astonishing to read that *one in five American adults is functionally illiterate* — that is, "incapable of understanding basic written and arithmetic communication to a degree that they can maneuver satisfactorily in contemporary society." And data from testing services bear out what community college, four-year college, and university instructors have been saying for at least a couple of decades: too many of their entering students are not sufficiently prepared for college level studies, academic or vocational.

Add to that the total number of immigrants — 700,000 legal and perhaps 300,000 illegal — who will enter this country annually in the future. Many will need education in the English language and other basic skills before they can enter job training programs or be acceptable for anything but the most menial employment. Mike Rose, who is associate director of UCLA Writing Programs, says this about remedial programs:

> At heart, the issue of remediation is embedded in two central questions: How is higher learning best pursued in a pluralistic democracy, and how many or how few do we want to have access to that learning? We are talking, finally, about the kind of society we want to foster.

VERY FEW COMMUNITY colleges offer classes for non-readers or for new immigrants who speak no English; such courses are found in adult education programs at high schools, in literacy programs at libraries, or elsewhere in the community. But just about all community colleges offer remedial or basic skills classes. Many offer whole programs with special support from counselors and tutors for students who, like Donald in the copy machine repair program, come to college so underprepared that they cannot immediately handle coursework leading to any certificate or degree.

But there are challenges to the open door concept that has been the heart of the community college philosophy. There is pressure for entrance standards. There is pressure to fund remedial classes at a lower rate than college-level classes. Only recently the U. S. Department of Education mandated that all new students to community colleges must hold a high school diploma or pass an aptitude test to screen their likely academic success. The law threatens colleges with the loss of federal financing (including funds for vocational education programs) if minimum enrollment standards are not met by all students.

Students must take an "Ability to Benefit" examination approved by the U. S. Department of Education before they matriculate if they hope to be eligible for financial aid. The Federal government has circulated a list of thirty-six approved ATB tests. In a survey of California community colleges, forty-seven colleges indicated that they had particular groups of students who failed whatever tests they were given: ESL students, students with learning disabilities, single parent/reentry students. And according to Linda Michalowski of the California Community College State Chancellor's Office, many students were scared off when informed of the testing process.

Placing ill-prepared students, many of whom are minorities, in remedial classes leaves community colleges open to charges of "tracking" or "cooling out," and such criticisms carry the word "racism" if the remedial English or math student also is counseled into vocational rather than transfer programs. But according to Troy Duster, a sociologist at the University of California at Berkeley and an African American, "unless you know a hell of a lot more about the processes by which students matriculate and move through the system, it is globally glib and of not much use to talk about racism.

"In general, I think that one has to be very alert to distinguish between purposeful, conscious action and inadvertent social outcomes," he said.

COMPONENTS OF ANY good vocational program are "options, constant evaluating, counseling, and mentoring," says Evan Dobelle, Chancellor/President of San Francisco City College. The college has a large airplane mechanic school out at the airport. "There are almost twenty thousand mechanics in the area," he says, "and we do a significant amount of the education of that group. And it's a good job. In two years, you can get a job at $30,000, and [the program can offer] one hundred percent employment to those who pass the test."

But students are not lock-stepped into any vocational program, and can change their minds midway through. Recently, he told us, one young man in the airplane mechanic program wanted to change direction, take another year of classes at the CCSF main campus and transfer to Berkeley to prepare for medical school. The counselors identified this student "because they're careful about it. Well, if he wants to be a doctor, I'm convinced he can do it. We're careful about how we do the vocational—it's not that we just assign you and you're forever at that career."

If this student had been enrolled in a high school occupations program which had exposed him to the world of airline mechanics, or to the world of medicine, he might not have dropped out of the collegiate level mechanic program to take up premed. More and more educators are suggesting that high school programs should combine academic subjects with concrete, work-related experiences, and that these secondary programs be carefully articulated with community colleges. Dale Parnell, former president of the American Association of Community and Junior Colleges, proposed what he called Two Plus Two Tech Prep programs, with high school students taking career courses in grades eleven and twelve and being assured that their units will count toward completion of a community college associate degree. An expansion of the Two Plus Two Tech Prep now in place in some community colleges is a very carefully articulated program in which students take both academic and career courses in grades eleven and twelve (including Principles of Technology or applied physics), and then move on to the community college to complete an associate degree in a career program and also complete the academic units needed to transfer to a four-year college.

Dobelle told us that he would expand the Two Plus Two concept even more. "I think the Two Plus Two programs are fundamental to the future of education, but beyond that, we have literature that has existed for eighty years now that suggests six-four-four systems, and yet we don't do anything about it," he says. He doesn't understand why "public education doesn't start two years earlier (at age three) when we know we're inheriting the problems that are affecting children at that age. And why community colleges don't expand and become four-year institutions and start with young people when they are sixteen and seventeen years old, in the last two years of high school."

It is not likely that in the near future public education will be restructured so that community colleges become four-year institutions and primary and secondary education will start two years earlier. But the Tech Prep programs are building bridges from high school programs to community college career programs and assuring students that they can go into the workforce or go on to four-year colleges, or both. With an associate degree, more than one door will be open to the future.

Eight

Big and Bold: Democracy's Colleges

*Every state should maintain as many Coledges in conveniant
parts thereof as would be attended upon to give the highest
Degrees of Larning . . . in the cheepest & best manner possible.*

— William Manning, *The Key of Libberty*

*The community colleges in the United States have been called
"democracy's colleges." They are probably the best known examples of a multi-purpose institution.*

— "Alternatives to Universities," 1991

As early as 1797, a Massachusetts farmer and tav-
ernkeeper, William Manning, wrote a book arguing for education as the only remedy against anti-democratic evils. Learning is of the greatest importance to the support of a free
government, he wrote, noting that the privileged few always
proclaim the advantages of costly colleges, national acada-
mies, and grammar schools, but always opposed what he
called cheap schools and woman schools, "the only or prin-
saple means by which learning is spred amongue the Many."

Today, the "few" do not oppose as much as they ignore.
Throughout this book we say that the community colleges are
not seen in proportion to their importance. Of course the men
and women who study or work on these campuses do not
underestimate the institutions. Nor do those suburban and
rural communities where the community college is often the
only institution of higher education within driving distance,

and the major learning center for the whole community. Anyone who has occasion to step onto a community college campus usually gets a sense of the people these schools serve and what they are about. The historian, Page Smith, spent his student and professorial life on university campuses, but he took such steps and says, "There are, I am sure, indifferent community colleges as well as good ones, but the ones I have visited have all charmed me, and I am pleased to have an opportunity to express my gratitude for the lively times and good spirit I have experienced in my visits."

For most policy- and imagemakers, however, and for many of the top spokespeople in higher education, these colleges, and maybe more importantly, their millions of students, hardly exist. They remain obscure abstractions.

When American Council on Education president Robert H. Atwell says "minority and low-income people go into community colleges from whence they are never seen," presumably he means that they never are seen at four-year colleges or universities, which is of course incorrect. But the remark implies that unless they are seen at four-year institutions, they do not exist anywhere; they are of no consequence. These millions of students are counted out, ignored, invisible.

Two-year colleges receive sparse mention in books on the history of education, and there is only one book-length history of the community college and that was written in 1931. Yet this is now the biggest system of higher education in the world. There are two major reasons why it is so often ignored: one is the populations served by community colleges; the other is their distinctive localness.

Many of the nearly six million students who enroll each year in credit courses are marginalized. They live, or at least they begin, on the outer boundaries of the inner circles. They are William Manning's "Many," and their needs and opportunities are deeply embedded in our history and values, and in the rhetoric that honors that history and those values. At the same time, however, a large part of the American political and commercial system has a strong tendency to look the other way when it comes to the real and practical needs and opportunities of these less affluent, less educated men, women, and children. We must hope this attitude is unwitting.

A good illustration comes from outside the educational world. Daily newspapers now systematically select news of interest to more affluent middle-class readers because those are the readers who attract advertising, and newspapers get seventy to eighty percent of their revenues from advertising. In the selection process, the concerns of this middle class — be it in taxes, jobs, inflation, income, or schooling — occupy most of the reporting and the rest fades. There is little or no systematic "beat" coverage of less upscale districts, of ghettos and working class neighborhoods and schools. University campuses frequently are part of a reporter's beat. Community college campuses rarely are.

There are, of course, occasional stories of tragic or heroic episodes but, except when in crisis, the daily concerns of ordinary working people, ordinary families in real situations are not what the more affluent middle class and most political leaders see day in and day out. People less affluent are scarcely visible in the depiction of what is important in society. Similarly un-visible is continuing information about their schooling, except for occasional complaints about its inadequacies.

Daily newspapers once served the whole spectrum of American families; now they consciously serve a smaller and smaller percentage of families. Increasingly, this has become true for magazines as well. To a lesser degree, this is also true of television, which aims for the same affluent audience. These media become both mirrors of who we are and lenses to what we see. They give each of us a sense of what is important in our own city, state, and nation. Our picture of the world is based in large part on what is emphasized in what we read and see day in and day out.

A related but somewhat different perspective comes from Dale Parnell, who was president of the American Association of Community and Junior Colleges when we spoke with him.

He told us that "the vast majority of people who write for the national press and television have not experienced a community college, and so it's very hard to explain to them who we are and what we're doing." He thinks it's going to help a lot "when there are more and more community college graduates placed in positions of leadership around the country," and he thinks we're getting there. He mentioned Robert Jones, Assistant Secretary of Labor in charge of the Job Partnership Training Act, with a $26 billion budget who, said Parnell, "just raves about his experiences" at Santa Barbara College.

His view is that "we will have arrived when the President of the United States has attended a community college and has an Associate degree up on the Oval Office wall."

A second major reason why public community colleges, their students, and their programs, are relatively invisible is their community-specific nature. They have the local quality of a neighborhood school, which is quite different from the prestige of a state university, with football teams that appear on television, winning or losing Rose Bowls, Orange Bowls, Cotton Bowls; with campaniles and monumental classic architecture; with graduates who become part of the identifiable power elite, or rich and famous.

"Big news" will rarely be made at these community colleges. They do not tackle national or world problems such as the rate of global warming, economic cycles, or quasars. The colleges are not research institutions. They produce no flood of academic publications or scientific breakthroughs. Their primary function is to teach students, and their students are from their communities.

They are local in many other ways, as well. We have described these colleges as part of the biggest system of higher education in the world, but the word "system" is misleading. In actuality, there are many systems. Governance and funding are often complex arrangements between state and local communities, arrangements that differ from state to state. In some states, individual districts are governed by local community boards that are elected in local elections. Sometimes a State

101

Board of Regents establishes general policy. In some states, their administration is part of the state university system. Recently, financial support and priorities seem to be moving from the local scene to the state capitol.

And not only are there significant differences among states. The colleges differ significantly from each other within the states. Each reflects its own community. Our own two colleges provide a telling illustration of the dramatic differences in the character of each college, even though they are only thirty-five miles apart.

Foothill College is situated atop a hill on the fringes of the suburban community of Los Altos Hills, where residential lots are an acre or more and many residents keep horses; a community public horse trail weaves through the campus. There are magnificent sweeping views of the mountains from every walkway. Low, redwood-sided buildings with wide eaves and shake roofs cluster around planted patios.

The college's service area is approximately eighty-three percent white, although the student body includes a higher ratio of racial and ethnic minorities. Of the 18,958 students who registered in the Winter Quarter of 1991, for instance, sixty percent were white, eleven percent Asian, six percent Mexican American/Latino, three percent African American, two percent other minorities, and eighteen percent other or unknown.

The towns that Foothill serves are suburban communities, spread out in what once were apricot orchards. Prestigious Stanford University is nearby. The area is economically dependent on electronics-oriented industries, and many of the workers in these industries commute from less-affluent areas. These workers are apt to be part-time Foothill students.

In contrast, a nine-story triangle of concrete topped by a green neon sign, "Laney College," is clearly visible from a freeway. The tower dominates a campus of two-story, red brick buildings separated by grey walkways. Although the campus sits next to a pleasant greensward and estuary of San

Francisco Bay and across the street from a first-rate municipal art museum, not far away are ethnic enclaves and the sprawl of a large seaport with industrial factories and shops. Within two blocks are a subway station, the Light of Buddha Temple, and the Open Door Mission bearing a sign, "Do Not Beg or Steal. Come Eat with Us."

Laney is one of four colleges in a district that serves six cities, of which the largest by far is Oakland. Two-thirds of its student body comes from Oakland, where more than forty percent of the population is African American. The city has been governed by African-American mayors, and until recently had the largest metropolitan American daily newspaper owned and edited by an African American. Close to one-fifth of the students come from the neighboring university city of Berkeley. About 10,800 students are enrolled.

In 1990, some seventy percent of Laney's student body was non-white: thirty-three percent African American; twenty-four percent Asian; ten percent Mexican American/Latino; and three percent other minorities. Only twenty-four percent was white, with six percent unknown. The average age of the whole student body was thirty-one.

LOCAL GOVERNANCE, LOCAL students, local needs. As we show throughout this book, each curriculum in some way reflects its parent community. Dairy Management is offered in an agricultural valley. Large numbers of courses in English as a Second Language are offered where new waves of immigrants are settling, whether this be in Florida, Texas, Arizona, or California. Many colleges offer reentry programs for women, non-credit courses for senior citizens, enrichment classes for anyone else in the community depending on need and demand—solar mechanics and bookbinding, Shakespeare and Italian for Travelers, computer programming and the Biology of AIDs. Each college has to keep reading its community as the community changes. San Francisco City College had the first Gay and Lesbian studies department in the country.

Miami-Dade College in Florida has the biggest foreign student population in higher education in the country. A plant closing led to the retraining program we describe in Chapter 7, and such programs in turn change the community.

Individual needs, community needs, and the college continually affect each other, and as a result community and college are in an ongoing process of change and evolution. The very localness of community colleges, and their ability to change and evolve in response to local needs makes for a fuzzy national visibility.

On the other hand, there are clearly defined shared and unique characteristics that cut across state and county differences. Public community colleges are almost always close to their students' homes; all are relatively inexpensive and open to all adults in their communities. And historically they all developed outside the vertical educational continuum that begins in kindergarten and ends with graduate school. They stand linked but separate. In that sense, these two-year colleges have always been alternative — although paradoxically this alternative is now being used by the majority of entering college students.

This unique positioning is closely linked to their bold and shared sense of mission. It has been restated in hundreds of ways by hundreds of different boards, administrations, and faculties.

Here it is in 1914 as the first public junior college in Oklahoma stressed industrial education in addition to college work: "Democracy is no new ideal for this country. Quite true, but we are coming to a larger social vision and a larger interpretation of democracy. We have long proclaimed the equality of our citizens, but we are coming to see that equality must mean equal opportunity for self-realization, recognition of individual differences. . . . "

Here it is in a 1950 statement of purpose for the Joliet (Illinois) Junior College by its governing School Board: "The American way of life holds that all human beings are supreme, hence of equal moral worth and are, therefore, entitled to equal opportunities to develop to their fullest capacities. The basic function of public education then should be to provide educational opportunity by teaching whatever needs to be learned to whoever needs to learn it, whenever he needs to learn it."

Such mission statements continue to be voiced by different community colleges in different states. The daily work on campuses is designed to put them into practice. The statements are lofty and idealistic, but the mission stays real and contemporary. It is big, bold, and, as William Manning reminds us, very American.

Nine

Keeping the Door Open: History and Change

The very essence of the egalitarian community college is rooted in the perception that no one is a second class citizen. To make everyone — part-time/full-time; older/younger; Anglo/minority; transfer/vocational; day student/night student feel that the community college is for them is no simple task. In all higher education, the community college is the only institution that even tries. I have come to believe that comprehensiveness is both the distinction and the challenge of the community college.

— K. Patricia Cross, 1990

Community colleges are a twentieth-century North American phenomenon. In the United States, they began as "junior" colleges, local and small, but they grew quickly in number and size, flourishing in the sixties and seventies: in Canada, many community colleges were developed and flourished in the same time period.

In those decades, alternatives to traditional universities expanded higher education in North America as well as in Europe, Japan, and New Zealand. "Admission to [post-secondary] levels of education and training in most national systems changed from a restrictive elite mode to varied patterns of mass higher education," reported the Organisation for Economic Co-operation and Development (OECD) in 1991. Most of the new systems were "more practically- and vocationally-oriented than the universities," but not all were alike. Three distinct models emerged.

One type was the "specialized" model which describes institutions that offer shorter, mostly vocationally-oriented courses in a limited number of areas, leading to below-first-degree level certifications. A large number of postsecondary institutions in continental Europe and Japan are close to this model.

Another type of institution, called the "binary" model, offers courses and certifications intended to be distinct from but of a comparable level to, those in universities. These post-secondary alternative institutions are typically represented by the British polytechnics.

A third model is the "multipurpose" institution, which, according to the OECD report, corresponds to the characteristics of most community colleges in the United States and Canada; it offers vocational courses and certification, the first two years of the four-year undergraduate degree, remedial work, and, increasingly, a wide range of continuing education.

In the United States, serious and influential support for the early "junior" colleges (not then the comprehensive community colleges of today) came at the turn of the century from educators such as William Rainey Harper, President of the University of Chicago, and then Alexis Lange, Dean of the School of Education at the University of California, and David Starr Jordan, President of Stanford University, who saw this new segment of higher education as a means to move their own universities away from the American "liberal arts college" and toward the specialization of the European research universities. They envisioned a coherent educational ladder, in which the first two years after high school were devoted to general education and personal development and the universities were then freed to offer advanced specialized studies and research. As far as we could discover, it was Harper who introduced the concept of the associate degree after successful junior college work.

Had the vision of these men been realized, our educational ladder would now look different. Junior colleges would have become the major link between high schools and universities.

But this did not happen except in rare instances. Colleges held on to their first two years, most universities did too—often for economic reasons just as much as educational reasons—and the junior college evolved, as we said earlier, linked but separate.

This unique positioning outside the vertical alignment of American formal education has been a source both of strength and vulnerability. As junior colleges grew in numbers and size, their mission evolved to include more and more programs that serve more and more people, the many functions we describe in previous chapters.

Universities and business and industry representatives understandably speak out in their own interests—preparatory training to enter the university, preparatory training to enter the workforce. These are legitimate functions of a community college. They are, however, single visions, blind or at least myopic to the multiple purposes of these schools and the multiple needs of their students.

Whether or not any one community college will continue to provide first, second, third chances for everyone, whether it can continue to permit students to try out, stop-out, shift directions, as need and times demand—the answer to these questions will be heavily influenced by public awareness and choices. The choices require clear vision, the ability to preserve a delicate balance among competing demands, and the ability to withstand powerful pressures.

SEVERAL FACTORS HAVE influenced the development of junior colleges from their early beginnings and continue to influence community college decisions today. Because these colleges are always within commuting distance and relatively inexpensive, they have attracted an ever-increasing number of students from increasingly diverse constituencies demanding access to higher education. During the same time period, many of the large public universities have moved farther and farther away from teaching as they put increasing emphasis on specialization and research. Another consistent and continuing factor is an ever-increasing technology that needs better trained men and women. In the early days we had the mechanization of agriculture; today we live with the electronic revolution.

The early junior college curriculum was two-thirds academic or college preparatory, although it is not at all clear how many students actually transferred. A 1937 study showed that seventy-five percent did not continue their education beyond the junior college, but this of course did not account for the zigzag pattern that seems to have characterized the educational pathways of many students even in those early days.

The 1930s brought the Great Depression followed by a World War, times that created new demands for occupational retraining and new careers. Few new colleges were founded during this period, but larger numbers of students were drawn to the ones already there, in spite of reduced state funding. By 1945, 315 public junior colleges were enrolling 216,325 students in credit courses.

A period of dramatic and horizontal development followed. After World War II, boosted by the GI Bill of Rights that offered free education to returning veterans and the 1947 Truman Commission Report that strongly supported the role of two-year colleges as equal opportunity institutions, more and more communities voted in their own new colleges.

It was the Truman Commission Report, titled *Higher Education for Democracy*, that suggested the name "community college."

> Only a few decades ago, high school education in this country was for the few. Now, most of our young people take at least some high school work, and more than half of them graduate from high school. Until recently college education was for the *very* few. Now a fifth of our young people continue their education beyond the high school. Many young people want less than a full four-year college course. The two-year college—that is, the thirteenth and fourteenth years of our educational system—is about as widely needed today as the four-year high school was a few decades ago. Such a college must fit into the community life as the high school has done.

109

Hence, the President's commission suggests the name "community college" to be applied to the institution designed to serve chiefly local community education needs. It may have various forms of organization and may have curricula of various lengths. Its dominant feature is its intimate relations to the life of the community it serves.

Or, as one college president put it, "We're not junior to anyone."

In the four decades following the end of World War II, the number of community colleges increased dramatically, from the 315 in 1945 to 975 in 1990. The numbers of students served increased even more dramatically, from the 216,325 in 1945 to nearly six million in credit courses in 1990, and probably another six million in non-credit courses.

The colleges were extending their invitation to education to a broader and broader spectrum of the community, some with clear goals and some with no goals but vague hopes: high school graduates (who came in droves during the sixties as the baby boom generation matured), some very able or gifted, some underprepared for collegiate work; high school drop-outs; middle-aged reentry women; laid-off workers; new immigrants; senior citizens. Curriculum changed to meet new community needs. Multi-cultural courses were added, as were women's studies programs, literacy programs, and English as a second language courses.

Vocational programs flourished—nursing, airplane mechanics, tractor repair, and many in the so-called High Technology fields. Many baccalaureate degree holders returned to the community college to get job training or take courses to prepare for new careers. Many colleges began to offer short-term training for certificates or proficiency—on campus or in partnership with local industry, as well as associate degrees in career training. Community services created a new wave of outreach, and began to offer enrichment classes for anyone in the community. Most of these do not offer college credit; many are supported by fees, not public funds.

Community college districts in large urban areas began adding second campuses, then third, fourth, or even more. Maricopa Community College District in Arizona now has ten; Los Angeles, nine; Chicago, eight; City University of New York, eight. The community college had become the widest invitation to higher education in the world.

THE ONGOING GIVE and take among student, community and college leads to a permanent feature of the community college: Change. One community college instructor who has taught at the same urban college for twenty-seven years showed us how such change is perceived by someone from within the institution:

> When I first started teaching, the community college where I was hired had just become comprehensive. It was a small vocational school just opening up a liberal-arts section. The students were mostly white lower class students, working class students. I was one of a bunch of brash, idealistic, and very liberal liberal-arts teachers and within a year or two we had doubled the number of faculty. And there were some real hostilities between vocational and liberal arts to be worked out. Looking back on it I can see why the vocational teachers were upset; they had a nice little school going, and all these little hotshots come down to take it away.
>
> But we worked it out. We learned to esteem one another. The vocational function of the community college is a part of its essence. The electrician who takes my American literature class because she loves to read and discuss ideas and the nursing student who needs to learn to write in complete sentences so that he can keep a coherent medical chart ground me as a teacher.
>
> And then civil rights came along, and we got a large black population. I had to learn how to teach all over again, which is why every time it's a different institution I had to learn.
>
> The key word was *relevance*. "What's the point of this? What does it have to do with my life?" they asked. To answer these new students I had to rethink the relevance and worth of the texts and methods with which I had been taught. And I had to

learn what I had not been taught—the literatures of African American, Hispanic, African, Native American peoples. I stopped lecturing; I learned to teach.

In the seventies, all sorts of wonderful students showed up on our campus—housewives, retirees, Vietnam veterans, hippies. Many of my students had advanced degrees and many of my students couldn't read above the sixth grade level. We celebrated our diversity in the classroom; the college became a great funky place, an open plaza of peoples.

The eighties brought us the new Asian immigrants. I learned to distinguish the names of Cambodian, Laotian, Vietnamese students. I learned not to assume that Hong Kong Chinese and Korean Chinese shared the same culture. I inwardly blushed as I explained to students who had been schooled to compose elegant essays of subtle allusion that in this barbarously brusque culture you are supposed to state exactly what you mean. I learned to appreciate being respected because I was the teacher.

When I first started at the community college I thought—I'll give myself seven years of teaching the semi-colon and *Hamlet* before I burn out. It has been twenty-seven years, and I'm not the least bit bored. And, who knows, there may be one or two more cycles left before I retire.

In one way or another, the shifts and changes that Carmen Rezendes describes from her own personal experience are confirmed by almost all demographic studies. The nation as a whole is undergoing similar shifts. In Texas, the minority population is forty-nine percent; California already has a majority of minorities in its schools, and in fact all major public school systems now have minority majorities. By the year 2000, demographer Harold Hodgkinson projects that "one of every THREE of us will be non-white." He then adds the astonishing statistic that two-thirds of the world's immigration and two-thirds of the people who change citizenship in the world come to the United States and that "of the 20 million new workers who will enter the work force between now and the year 2000, 82 percent will be female, non-white or immigrant."

Hodgkinson concludes that "it is also clear that for the next decade, the only growth area in education will be in adult and continuing education" and that those students "whose needs are compatible with what the campus environment encourages" tend to stay in college. In a subsequent study, he adds that "research now makes it very clear that having college-graduate parents is the best single thing you can do to guarantee success in education yourself."

TWO STRONG STRANDS that converged in the founding of the very early junior colleges deserve a closer look. One is the thinking and writing of influential university educators who hoped to free their universities from lower division work, leaving "senior" colleges closer to the specializing function of the German university system.

This strand has been passed down in the literature. Men like William Rainey Harper (Chicago), Alexis Lange (University of California), and David Starr Jordan (Stanford) are usually credited with "inspiring" or "initiating" the junior college movement, even with "founding" the early colleges.

A second, independent, equally powerful strand traces the roots of these early colleges more to the efforts by local citizens who wanted to offer collegiate education and training to un-affluent local students who lived too far away to attend state colleges and universities; they worked to get bond issues passed, boards organized, facilities built, staffs hired, accreditations met. These early beginnings are still largely unexplored territory.

Two strong traditions are at play here, two points of view that have been with us for a long time: one looks at how ideas create and influence our social, political, and economic realities. The other looks at how human needs and demands (which in turn grow out of social and political and economic realities that touch people's lives) generate ideas. What was their relationship at any moment in history? What is their relationship now?

The questions are worth pursuing, especially since these two strands often emerge as conflicting points of view in the current debates on what the community college is and where it should be headed. But for our purposes here, it seems enough to say that over the years these two strands merged. Ideas cogwheeled with local demands to become the junior college, and then the community college system as we now know it.

But it is also significant that the particular origins of individual colleges can be found in the efforts of local men and women who had their faces turned to the communities in which they lived, and that this historical segment is fading in the literature about community colleges. Why is this significant? Because the impetus was so drastically different. The goal of one group was wider inclusion. The primary goal of the other, greater exclusion.

"A real community demand" led to Goshen Junior College in Indiana (c. 1904) according to Victor Hedgepeth, Superintendent of Goshen's public schools. "Local demand in the evening college" led to the first public junior college in Massachusetts (1917). Wyoming did not found its first junior college until 1945, in this case against the active opposition of its university, but with strong local support. In 1944, a delegation from Casper that included local businessmen and community leaders called for comprehensive junior colleges "supported by local taxes and tuition that would provide low-cost adult education, transfer education, vocational and general education for all the local citizens including the large number of returning veterans."

The vigor comes from the ground up. It affirms the story this country tells itself—that education and opportunity are available to all its citizens.

In contrast, the over-arching ideas that provide a conceptual framework for what became known as the junior college movement reveal a different impetus: to protect the interests of the universities and the education of the few. President Ray Lyman Wilbur of Stanford University referred to junior colleges as "shock absorbers." When David Starr Jordan of Stanford urged "the amputation of freshman and sophomore classes to prevent university atrophy" and to provide "relief to the university," he implied new groups of students demanding higher education, students the university wanted to be relieved of.

The point here is not that these were particularly callous men. They weren't. As long as they could protect their universities from the ever-increasing number of high school graduates, they were not adverse to opening different educational opportunities for these new graduates. By many accounts, they were inspiring educational pioneers.

The point is that when influential men (and women) — be they from education, from business, from government — are practically divorced from the people and institutions they are affecting, when they don't "know" them in any real sense of the word, then those people and institutions are in danger of becoming humanly invisible, no matter how conceptually real.

Recently, we found ourselves in conversation with an editor of a major west coast newspaper. He is noted for his liberal views, yet he argued with great certitude that given the shrinking financial pie, community colleges should spend their money on the more predictable successes, the worthier students, not on the failures who drop out. But those words — "drop-out" and "failure" — are loaded words. They lose meaning when we don't actually know what students interrupt their schooling and when and why, and who drops back in and when and why.

Ideas can distort even in the face of experience. One community college critic, proud of his skepticism, visited Miami-Dade Community College after it had been named number one in the country. Wanting to apply his "critic's perspective," he writes he "would try to be thorough and fair, tough-minded of course."

He goes, he sees, he is conquered. He returns "impressed and shaken" at all that had been accomplished by faculty, administrators, and staff. But he concludes by describing their work as "their commitment to doing a little bit of God's work." His concluding imagery implies a conceptual frame that is at odds with the experience he describes (and with experience as we know it). He has visited a colony. The professional becomes the missionary and the student becomes the native in need of saving.

In higher education generally, students must fit themselves to the programs and timetables of the schools. What distinguishes the community college universe from all others in higher education, what has characterized it from its beginnings, is a powerful and unique idea: each college is to develop courses and programs to meet the needs of its community and its students—day or evening, one course or five courses, remedial or transfer, job retraining or job upgrading.

In David's words, "You don't have to fit into *it*; you can make it fit into your life."

Ten

Community College Issues:
What Is Success?

A lot of people just have this longing and at some point in their lives say, "OK, I want to go for something better."

— David Mullen, 1988

Working on this book, we have noted again and again how the lives of many people, perhaps most people, constantly take new directions. Life histories rarely are "efficient." They do not progress along straight, predetermined paths. And everything predicted about our futures, particularly our future working lives, suggests that change will be a constant. It is important that along the way in these life histories there be possibilities of positive new beginnings. This belief in the ability to make new beginnings, we think, lies at the heart of the democratic promise.

Certainly the possibility of new beginnings is at the heart of the mission of community colleges, and that's why they have been called "springboards" and "safety nets." As springboards, they permit students to move upward in their aspirations. As safety nets, they offer assurances to those who have had little opportunity for higher education and are timid about trying.

The overriding issue for this decade is whether community colleges will be able to sustain that compound mission through the difficult nineties and the unknowns of the next century. Will they be able to keep their multiple functions, their close ties to their communities, to be comprehensive enough and flexible enough to change as needs change? Supremely, will they be able to preserve the central principle of their mission, to be open to all?

Looking at the lives of real students illuminates the importance of how these policy questions get answered. One new adult student writes: "I've wanted to study and earn a degree that will allow me to make a contribution even when I was in high school. I just never really thought it was possible for someone like me to do. For years I imagined I'd be a cowboy, or a carpenter, or a diver. But never a student. You see, besides thinking that I might not have the right amount of grey matter to get good grades, I thought that I was alone in the world with my dream to get a degree. None of the people I've been around much of the past 10 years aspire to such things. To find out that others have had the same feelings is, what's the word, liberating."

And it is not just the inadequately prepared students who find new beginnings. Henry Louis Gates, Jr., the distinguished literary critic and historian, entered a Virginia community college as a premed student. An English teacher at the college, Duke Anthony Whitmore, caused him to change his life plan. "Duke made the study of literature, and the art of composing essays, seem as delicious as the corn-on-the-cob that my Uncle Jim used to pitchfork out of the cast iron tub at the Colored Labor Day Mill Picnic in Mineral County in the fifties," said Gates. "And it was that marvelous experience which shaped my entire, subsequent existence and led me to my career as a critic and scholar of African and African-American studies."

It is the reality of students' lives that makes us increasingly wary of proposals that come from serious and well-intentioned scholars and analysts who do not take these actualities into account. To be sure, they look at real problems — budget problems, the need for some standards, and other impersonal factors. And of course we need analytical studies that find patterns across populations. The problem is that often such studies obscure and homogenize the variety. Because they apply to everybody, they apply to nobody. We have made students prominent in this book because we believe a plan that does not begin with the lives and needs of the people affected is inadequate, no matter how rational or efficient sounding. The map must fit the territory.

It is for this reason that we argue so strongly for the comprehensive mission of the community college, the multiple purpose campus. But across the country, pressures are growing for change. With public four-year institutions eliminating classes, raising tuitions, and setting earlier application deadlines, the overflow comes to the community colleges. And as community colleges suffer budget cuts, as more four-year students crowd into community colleges, more of the students who are less academically prepared, or do not yet know what they hope to accomplish, are being squeezed out.

Florida and North Carolina community colleges already have limited their enrollment or are preparing to do so. At North Carolina's Central Community College, 1991 tuition increased by fifty-three percent, and President Marvin Joyner worried about the disproportionate effect on minorities and low-income students. California still has the lowest tuition in the country, but is limiting the number of basic skills courses a student may take.

Fearsome budgetary restraints now descending on all public education are forcing colleges to establish priorities. Under that pressure, the temptation is great to concentrate more on the easy "successes," on the educationally better prepared students, and to shorten the expected time in which a student must complete a given program. Increasingly, funding gets tied to quantitative measures and standardized achievements. Remedial funding is reduced.

There is danger in applying the wrong standards or too rigid a yardstick to community colleges. They, like their students, don't fit neatly into conventional educational slots. Their strength, like that of their students, has been the ability to be adaptable and flexible, in the colleges' cases, to the changing needs of their own communities. Economic crises and industrial shifts bring about new programs, as do waves of immigration, as do changed requirements at their neighboring four-year schools. In the big picture, the direction of each college both follows and helps bring about the changes within each community.

It is urgent that we look at the colleges as they really exist. Times now are volatile. There has been a downward drift in educational funding at the same time that the public demands more education, not less. In this uncertainty and change, decision-makers both within community colleges and outside the institutions need to be clear on what is at stake.

IN THE ONGOING debates over community college, the central issue once again is "mission"—how to define the purpose and goals of the system. As we describe in Chapter 8, community college mission statements have been rewritten over the years; most dramatic was the GI Bill and the subsequent expansion of all higher education which led to the move from junior college to community college, the widening door for occupational programs. Colleges today, trying to figure out how to continue within budgetary restraints, are considering possible new sources of support; financial imperatives are thus forcing a re-examination that may take the colleges into new directions.

We do not argue against change. That is inevitable. We do argue that it is dangerous to abandon the comprehensive mission, to shrink or slide back to being junior colleges that attune themselves primarily to students who come prepared and with clear academic goals in mind. If that should happen, millions of potential community college students who are not yet academically proficient and so do not yet have a clear goal would be closed out.

The most serious threats to the comprehensive mission have come from those who want to elevate a single function at the expense of all others. With occupational programs expanding on most campuses, one response has been to embrace this new direction toward careers. Advocates would firmly restructure community colleges as career education institutions, offering both two-year career programs and undergraduate work leading to transfer into baccalaureate career programs. Thus liberal arts transfer programs might be sacrificed, but not all transfer functions would be given up.

Darrell Clowes and Bernard Levin, the former a university professor, the latter a community college instructor, summarized the position of those who would elevate the career function above others. "The community, technical and junior college must identify a core function and restructure itself around that core function. We believe career education is the viable choice. . . . A modified transfer and collegiate function could develop from this core and could provide the basis for maintaining some position within higher education. The remaining functions could become satellites to the core of career education: remedial education would be a necessary and appropriate support activity."

Most frequently heard, however, are recommendations to make transfer the sovereign function of the community college. Here, advocates come from differing political directions. From one side, the argument insists that these colleges are spreading themselves too thin, that by trying to serve the entire population, they shortchange everybody. They hope to "restore" the institution to what it "should be." Following this route, community colleges would revert to being truly *junior* colleges, less tied to the needs of their local populations, more focused on the courses and programs designed to send students on to four-year colleges and universities. Since transfer education is considerably less expensive than occupational and remedial programs, this option is especially attractive in days of budget cuts.

Another audible group for change would by-pass non-transfer programs in the name of egalitarianism. These critics see occupational and vocational courses and the like as undemocratic, denying minority and low-income people a chance at entering the mainstream four-year college by limiting their sights to working-class jobs. As one such critic put it, "Access broadly defined must include the baccalaureate degree if two-year colleges are to avoid contributing to the creation of a permanent underclass."

As we've suggested before, social mobility is a major issue in almost all debates about the primacy of the transfer function, but there is a serious question about how much any one institution can do to change patterns of group mobility and singlehandedly bring about a more classless society. Such a goal would need national support and the concerted efforts of all educational segments.

Arthur Cohen and Florence Brawer point out this difficulty when they note the difference "between equalization and equal access, between overturning the social class structure and allowing people to move from one stratum to another." They argue that "if equal opportunity means allowing people from any social, ethnic, or religious group to have the same chance to enter higher education as people from any other group, the goal is both worthy and attainable. And few would question the community college's contribution to the breaking down of social, ethnic, financial, and geographical barriers to college attendance. But when that concept is converted to *group* mobility, its meaning changes, and it is put beyond the reach of the schools."

Both of these arguments—to restore the collegiate function as the central function, or to bring the baccalaureate within immediate reach of all students—both of these "positions" are heavily based on ideology, not on the reality of people's lives as they are actually lived in thousands of different communities. And they are not based on knowledge of how men and women in ordinary life actually advance in education.

It is patronizing for graduates with higher degrees to tell others that degrees are not necessary. But it is also patronizing for graduates with higher degrees to cast the world in their own image and demand the same path and the same credentials for everyone else. Allowing that accurate numbers are hard to come by and their interpretation notoriously unreliable, a fairly low percentage of incoming community college students name the baccalaureate as their *principal* destination. Having access to a multi-function community college, however, gives these same men and women a chance eventually to make it their principal destination.

When decision makers rely primarily on standardized achievements that can be measured by numbers, they exclude thousands of adults in the name of "excellence" and efficiency. In a multiple function institution, dimensions of success are not easily expressed in simple or universal hard numbers. Moreover, the overall statistics that carry so much weight with legislators and other policymakers are often dubious in their accuracy, contain large and confusing gaps, and so can be used selectively to support almost any predetermined point.

GIVEN TODAY'S POLITICAL climate, positions easily become polarized. Supporting the multiple function campus can be depicted as racism, wanting to hold back minorities. On the other hand, supporting an elevated transfer function can be depicted as elitism. Somewhere in between is the thinking of someone like Evan Dobelle, San Francisco City College's Chancellor, who talks about the transfer function as the major function — "community colleges are colleges," he says, "and the goal should be the baccalaureate." But not, he then adds, to the exclusion of vocational or of remedial education. Each student, he feels, *should* have the goal of the baccalaureate for his or her own education as a citizen, and because "there is great merit in having a culturally literate society." But that doesn't mean a linear progression of four years, or five or six. Dobelle earned his own baccalaureate degree *after* a special masters, when he was thirty-eight years old. An interrupted pattern is not only acceptable in his view. Sometimes it is essential.

"Major function," however, still implies a giant, if not among pygmies, at least among those of lesser stature, and it is the fear of many that the real consequences will be exclusion. Patricia Cross notes that no other sector in American education so conscientiously serves a clientele with such different destinations.

"To overemphasize the transfer function," she says, "would serve best those students who already lead in the educational pipeline. The same pressure that keeps transfer students moving impedes experimentation, discourages stopouts and the non-traditional patterns of entry and re-entry that characterize the majority of community college students. Determining the right kind and amount of pressure to improve the transfer function and yet permit exploration by the majority of adult students in the community college is ... a delicate matter."

WE AGREE THAT attention needs to be paid to the critical concern that community colleges do not send *enough* students to the four-year colleges or universities (although they do better than critics claim). A major problem of a too theoretical approach, however, is the unreliability of existing numbers. Numbers vary widely: from five percent to forty-two percent or more. James Palmer, former Director of Data Collection and Policy Analysis for the AACJC, told us that "there isn't a week goes by that somebody doesn't call me up—usually from the press—and says, 'Jim, what's the transfer rate from community colleges to four-year colleges?' The answer is, to be very honest, we don't know.

"It's one thing," he says, "to count the number of students sitting in the classes at any one time. [But] if you were to ask most community colleges, 'How many of your former students transferred to neighboring universities, and of those students, how many got bachelor degrees?' they could not tell you. All sorts of problems here: universities don't cooperate with the community colleges. A student may take a year's worth of courses at a community college, work for three years, and then end up at a university somewhere, and that tie-in is not made. We just don't know. The data are very slim." Cohen and Brawer confirm that "no one knows what the transfer numbers for the nation truly are."

Palmer thinks that "if you want to take a look at the community college role in baccalaureate education, it's better to take a look backward and figure that out. . . . Suppose," he says, "we were able to take all the bachelor degree recipients in a given year, and track their records backwards to how many of them had transferred credits from a community college." Then the numbers change radically. In California, the conventional wisdom has been citing the transfer rate at five percent. But over fifty-one percent of the 47,459 students who graduated from the California State University system in 1989, and over twenty-one percent of the 26,261 students who graduated from the University of California system in 1990, had "transferred from the California Community Colleges."

Similar numbers are reported in the state of Washington. In 1988, forty-eight percent of the students who graduated from regional state colleges and twenty percent who graduated from the University of Washington with bachelor degrees had transferred credits from community colleges. At Arizona State University, forty-four percent of upper division students transferred from community colleges. In Florida, seventy-six percent of the minority students within the state university system began their education at a community college.

Palmer thinks that "until we get better data, all arguments about how good is the community college function will be tendered by political considerations. . . . If you want to take a look at the community college role in baccalaureate education, it's better to take a look backward and figure that out."

Another problem with data is how each college or system counts its transfer students. What number will become the denominator, the total against which the percentage is figured? If all students who enroll are counted, then the percentage will be very low; if only the full-time students who declare transfer as their goal are counted, the percentage will be considerably higher.

Even then, the way the question is asked, the pressure on students to declare a "goal" at registration, makes for unreliable data. Alison Bernstein of the Ford Foundation hopes for greater reliability by including in the pool only the "student who has completed more than 18 degree credit hours of community college work." But neither this nor any other system has been adopted nationally as a way to count potential transfer students. Data collection is not standardized.

The Ford Foundation has given grants to twenty-four urban community colleges in an effort to bolster the transfer rate of underrepresented students. Funds were used on campus to schedule regular meetings with representatives from four-year schools, to establish resource centers that make available catalogues and other information, to hold classes that deal with time management and study skills, and to initiate honors programs. Funds were also used off campus to establish closer cooperation with high schools. The beginning of LaGuardia's Middle College High School (see p. 39) was in part supported by Ford money. Ford funding was for three years only, but many of the colleges have been able to continue some of these programs on their own. Again, hard numbers don't exist, but there is a general consensus that the Transfer Opportunity Programs created a climate for transfer on community college campuses and stimulated four-year schools to coordinate efforts. However, the question remains: Do working-class and minority students stand a lesser chance of getting a baccalaureate if they enter a community college?

A frequently cited study by A. W. Astin of the University of California at Los Angeles says just that: that the student who goes to a community college has less chance to complete a bachelor's degree than a student who starts in a four-year college, even when allowing for all sorts of factors like academic ability and socio-economic status.

As we see it, the problem with that study, published in 1977, assumes that the student has a choice between entering a two-year college or a four-year college, and ignores the fact that for many students, the choice is between entering a community college or not entering any college at all.

The Astin study, however, does raise the question of what can be done institutionally to help students stay in school.

There is confirming evidence, for instance, that living on a campus, attending full-time, perhaps holding a campus job, are factors that help keep a student in school. By those measures, community colleges, very few of which have dormitories, are a failure by definition. But given the average age of the community college student—twenty-nine—and the fact that most students have some kind of job off campus, it seems unlikely that residence halls would by themselves provide the collegiate environment that could help keep them in school.

More relevant to community colleges are programs where students spend more hours per week with each other and with their instructors, like the block programs described in Chapter 4. This is surprisingly true for vocational programs that are often classified as "terminal." Students share goals, and as one instructor told us, "They're not just going to school, they're going to *be* something." Classes frequently are smaller, and students usually stay with the same group, sometimes for as long as two or three years, with frequent assessment and evaluation of students' progress, and carefully supervised workplace learning situations.

What this adds up to is less anonymity and isolation for both instructors and students, greater coherence and frequent feedback, closer relationships over a longer period of time, smaller groups, and hands-on experience, all of which do lead to a greater likelihood of academic aspirations and achievement.

TRANSFER IS UNQUESTIONABLY one of the chief functions of a community college. Even the American Association of Community Colleges, committed as it is to the concept of multiple mission, declared 1991 The Year of Transfer. But transfer is not the clear-cut and separate track that it is often made out to be. The curriculum line between vocational education and transfer education is very blurred. And with few exceptions, career programs at today's community college have counterparts at four-year institutions.

The most popular vocational programs—engineering, business, and health care—require "academic" prerequisites;

Connie's course in microbiology (Chapter 2) is listed and numbered as a collegiate transfer course, but she enrolled because it was required for her RN program, a vocational program. And there is a stronger demand by employers for students with academic education (especially in communications), as well as career certificates or degrees. Just as some students use vocational courses or programs to prepare for transfer, some also use academic courses to upgrade job skills, particularly business and computer courses.

The United States Department of Education confirms this reality. It no longer makes a distinction between associate degrees granted in occupational areas and associate degrees in academic areas leading to transfer. Today, the department reports data on associate degrees by subject area only.

A MAJOR CAUSE for our concern is that the push for a transfer-oriented community college brings with it the specter of admission requirements, which would mean closing the open door. It can be closed directly by pre-testing applicants and admitting only those who are likely to succeed, overtly screening out those deemed "unqualified." Of course it can also be closed indirectly by admitting all applicants, but offering only scattered courses or programs for the less prepared, making no systematic effort to help them attain or maintain collegiate level skills. Both ways would in effect annul the comprehensive community college that admits a wide variety of students and offers them various courses and pathways. Up to now, the principle has been inclusion, not exclusion.

Again, this principle of inclusion does not mean that today there are no tests or prerequisites. Placement tests are used to determine appropriate level of assignment to classes like arithmetic, algebra, trigonometry, or calculus. Almost universally, students need to test into freshman English courses, either by writing an essay or getting a specified score on a standardized test. To enter the LVN program, Connie had to pass a test in English and math; to enter the RN program she had to show satisfactory completion of a microbiology course and one in anatomy and physiology.

Ultimately, all the above considerations lead to a fairly simple question: How do we define success for community college students and programs? The answer to that question reveals the way the mission is perceived and will influence educational policy decisions for the rest of this decade.

The standard measure of educational success still looks at whether a student earns a degree, transfers to another campus, or completes a certificate, usually within a limited number of years. Community colleges have inherited this inadequate measure from the four-year college system. It is a thirteenth- and fourteenth-grade junior college concept of linear progression and ignores the reality of our student population, and the real circumstances in adult society. We need a new measurement of "success."

John Losak, Dean of Institutional Research at Miami-Dade College, asks for a redefinition. He argues that "all of the comparative studies use university-oriented success criteria and timelines, and fail to consider the several missions of community colleges." He defines a successful student as one who graduates, or remains enrolled in good academic standing, or leaves college in good academic standing.

We agree. In fact, his redefinition seems to apply equally to four-year institutions these days. A recent study by the Educational Testing Service indicated that of the top high school graduates entering college, fewer than half complete baccalaureate degrees within seven years, and the number is decreasing.

Transfer and career programs are centrally important to community colleges, and they earn us credibility. But they are not the only important goals. Our mission is broader. In the words of McCabe, it is "to provide an education program to raise the quality of life in our communities." Community colleges do not ignore the four out of five American adults who do not hold a baccalaureate degree. And even with a

129

dramatic growth of baccalaureate degree holders, says Dale Parnell, past president of the AACJC, at least three out of four students in the public schools are unlikely to achieve a baccalaureate degree.

We want to see community colleges remain comprehensive with their several functions intertwined. We want to see the colleges remain flexible enough to adapt to, but not be controlled by, new conditions such as the increased enrollments of baccalaureate-bound students just out of high school who opt to postpone university entry when tuition and fees are rising. We want to see them teach critical thinking to occupational students and to welcome industry's support of such instruction. We want them to continue to welcome adult students who lack academic preparation for collegiate work, and to offer them that second and third chance to succeed. Faculty and staff seem to agree.

Multi-function community colleges offer no guarantee of individual success, of economic security, or of civic stability. No education alone can do this. Without these colleges, however, hundreds of thousands of men and women will not be able to acquire or upgrade their job skills, like the bookkeeper who wants to become an accountant or the assembly line worker who wants to become a machinist. They will not be able to look for enrichment, like the court reporter who regularly takes one non-business course a semester. They will not be able to learn to read better or broaden their own narrow interests, maybe learn Spanish, like one "stop-out" who returns to his college now and then to become proficient in the language he uses in a community volunteer project.

When men and women like Connie, David and David's Aunt Minnie, Joe, Patricia, and Daniel first enrolled as community college students, they would have appeared directionless, without clear-cut goals, often uncomfortable with academic culture. All of them, however, were able to write their own educational scripts to become what they have become:

oncological nurse, future educator, rehabilitation facility director, computer technician, lawyer, copy machine repairman.

Pressures on community colleges to straighten or shorten the paths of their millions of students, pressures to limit their comprehensive offerings and close their open doors, jeopardize the work of these colleges. This threatens many of their students with what may be the most dangerous social and personal phenomenon: an absence of hope.

The genius of the community colleges is that it is the only established national system that is open to all adult Americans who want to advance their education, increase their occupational skills, enrich their intellectual and cultural life. It is the only established national system that serves as both springboard and safety net for the inevitable millions who wish to move upward as well as those who missed earlier opportunities and are ready to try anew.

Notes

Introduction

xii *We are worried about what will happen to them.* According to *The Chronicle of Higher Education*, Nov. 6, 1991, p. A1, A38. "for the first time in at least 33 years, state governments appropriated less money for higher education this year than last." Many states gave a priority this year to community colleges and student aid, but as Gerald W. Christenson, Chancellor of the Minnesota Community College System, said, "We're really pressed to try to deal with the large increases [in enrollment] and community colleges always operated on a frugal funding base."

xii *It is why a recent international commission. Alternatives to Universities* (Paris, France: Organisation for Economic Co-operation and Development, 1991), p. 37.

Chapter 1. The New Educational Reality

1 *Harry S. Truman, 1950.* From a letter written in 1950 to the Hon. Oscar R. Ewing, Administrator, Federal Security Agency. Quoted in Thomas Diener, *Growth of An American Invention: A Documentary History of Junior and Community Colleges* (New York: Greenwood Press, 1989), p. 131.

1 *Nearly half the students enrolled.* According to *The Chronicle of Higher Education Almanac* (August 26, 1992), p. 3, forty-six percent of the 10,740,540 enrolled in public institutions of higher education are enrolled in public two-year colleges. At public four-year institutions, minorities make up 17.3 percent of the total enrollment; at public two-year institutions, 22.5 percent.

1   *They are not all age eighteen to twenty-two.* Of the twelve million students enrolled in college in 1985, only one in six was full-time, in residence, and between eighteen and twenty-two years of age. Harold L. Hodgkinson, *All One System: Demographics of Education — Kindergarten Through Graduate School* (Washington D.C.: Institute for Educational Leadership, 1985), p 10.

1   *Nearly six million American adults.* The American Association of Community and Junior Colleges estimates the Fall, 1990, headcount enrollment to have been 5,701,727, with 3,774,569, or sixty-six percent, attending part-time. *A Summary of Selected National Data Pertaining to Community, Technical and Junior Colleges*, American Association of Community and Junior Colleges. (Washington, D. C., June 1991, unpublished), p. 11.B.1.

2   *Their average age is twenty-nine.* Arthur M. Cohen and Florence B. Brawer, *The American Community College*, Second Edition (San Francisco: Jossey-Bass, 1989), p. 32.

2   *"This pattern of ad hoc attendance."* Cohen and Brawer, p. 57.

3   ... *workers will have as many as three careers. Building Communities: A Vision for a New Century*, A Report of the Commission of the Future of Community Colleges (Washington D. C., AACJC, 1988), p. 22.

3   ... *three-fourths of all jobs. Building Communities*, p. 20.

3   ... *more than five-sixths of those entering the workforce.* William B. Johnston, *Workforce 2000: Work and Workers for the 21st Century* (Indianapolis: Hudson Institute, 1987).

3   *Public community colleges number nearly one thousand.* Here is a good example of how difficult it is to get accurate numbers. In 1988, the American Association of Community and Junior Colleges (AACJC) was officially using the number 1,068. In 1991, the AACJC listed 975 and said, "The number of public colleges shows a decline because different criteria were used to count. Only individually accredited colleges were counted. Private college numbers increased because tribally controlled colleges were added

to this category." *A Summary of Selected National Data*, p. 11.A.1. *The Chronicle of Higher Education Almanac* (August 26, 1992), p. 3, listed 968 public two-year colleges. Adding up the listings in AACJC's *The Times* (August 25, 1992), pp. B2–B10, we total 990. Note that the 1992 AACJC's *Times'* data on community college credit enrollment differs from the 1992 *Almanac's* data: AACJC *Times*, 5,956,914; *Almanac*, 4,937,663.

3   *South Dakota.* Because listings differ, we confirmed this number by telephone with the Regents' Office in South Dakota. Nationally, there are twenty-three tribal colleges supported by federal funds and private endowments.

3   *Five million in non-credit courses.* This is a "guess" made by James C. Palmer, former Director of Data Collection and Policy Analysis, AACJC, in an 1989 interview. According to Palmer, "the Federal Government does not collect data on students in non-credit or continuing education courses," and the data collected by the AACJC "are notoriously bad simply because there are no standards. . . . non-credit programming varies from offering a concert on campus to an actual class with learning objectives and tests." He estimates that approximately the same number of students enroll in non-credit courses as in credit courses.

3   *The cost per term.* National figures based on 1992 data in the *Almanac*, p. 3.

7   *In recent years.* Allan Bloom, *The Closing of the American Mind: How Higher Education Has Failed Democracy and Impoverished the Souls of Today's Students* (New York: Simon and Schuster, 1987), pp. 22, 344.

Chapter 2. David and Connie: Writing Their Own Educational Scripts

8   *Mary Catherine Bateson. Composing a Life* (New York: The Atlantic Monthly Press, 1989), p. 2.

15 *Of the twenty million new workers.* Harold L. Hodgkinson, "Whatever Happened to the Norman Rockwell Family?" *The Changing American Family.* Ninth Annual Providence Journal/Brown University Public Affairs Conference (March 1–16, 1989), p. 9.

15 *According to a 1989 census report.* U. S. Bureau of the Census, Current Population Reports, Series P-20, No. 451, *Educational Attainment in the United States: March 1989 and 1988* (Washington D.C., U. S. Government Printing Office, 1991), pp. 1, 57.

17 *At community colleges nationally.* Cohen and Brawer, p. 32.

Chapter 3. Community College Students: Diverse Goals, Diverse Paths

18 Edmund J. Gleazer, Jr., *The Community College: Values, Vision, and Vitality* (Washington, D. C.: American Association of Community Colleges, 1980) p. 8.

19 *Officially speaking.* See Cohen and Brawer, pp. 16–19.

20 "*. . . this pattern of ad hoc attendance.*" Cohen and Brawer, p. 57.

20 *Take for example, Patricia Keller.* Patricia was one of six former students of Foothill College, Los Altos, CA, who spoke to an Opening Day faculty meeting in September, 1984, with Ann Connor in attendance. Their stories of what Foothill meant to them were videotaped and are on file in the Learning Center.

21 *Or consider Elaine Dormshield.* One of the six former students mentioned above.

22 *In Wisconsin, Joe D.* Joe's story was told to us by a former teacher, Lyle Wanless, at Wisconsin Area Technical College in an interview, April 29, 1988.

22 *The average student age.* Cohen and Brawer, pp. 32, 34.

22 *In 1991, only three in ten.* AACC, "Statistical Brief," Annual Fall Surveys, Full-time and Part-time Enrollment, Fall 1980–Fall 1991, pp. 58–61.

23 *In some respects, Dina Rasor.* One of the Foothill six mentioned above.

23 *John Davidson, like Dina.* John was interviewed for us by Alma Oberst Holmgren, a journalist and former community college journalism instructor, in Denver in 1990.

24 *Dina and John were pretty sure.* Cohen and Brawer, p. 49.

25 *Miami is the city. The World Almanac and Book of Facts 1990* (New York, Newspaper Enterprise Association, Inc., 1989), p. 702.

26 *Miami-Dade's majority.* Cohen and Brawer, p. 43.

26 *Minority students constitute. The Chronicle of Higher Education 1992 Almanac*, p. 3. The 1991 AACJC data *Summary*, p. 11.C.3, says, "In terms of higher education as a whole, minorities are more likely to attend community, technical, and junior colleges than are whites. Enrolling only 36 percent of the nation's white college students, community colleges enroll 59 percent of Native American college students, 56 percent of Hispanic college students, 42 percent of all black college students,and 40 percent of all Asian college students."

26 *But all colleges share a mandate. Building Communities*, p. 6.

27 *James Edward Oberst (called Jim Ed).* Interviewed by Alma Oberst Holmgren in Lexington, Kentucky, in 1990.

29 *Time magazine described it. Time* (February 27, 1989), pp. 10–11.

Chapter 4. Builders of Community, Agents of Change

30 *The Commission on the Future of Community Colleges* from *Building Communities: A Vision For a New Century* (Washington, D. C.: American Association of Community and Junior Colleges, 1988), p. 7.

34 *The City Colleges of Chicago.* Mary Lou Santorec, editor, *Recruitment and Retention in Higher Education*, 4 (Madison, WI.: Magna Publications, Inc., March 1990), p. 4.

35 *Miami-Dade Community College.* Interview with Robert McCabe.

36 *Miami-Dade started the first group.* Telephone interview with Marvell Smith, Program Director, December 18, 1991.

38 *(About thirty-one percent). The World Almanac and Book of Facts* (1991), p. 564.

42 *"Our job is to get the message out." The Chronicle of Higher Education,* August 5, 1992, p. A14.

43 *This two-year "test" program. Innovation,* XIX (Laguna Hills, CA, September 1991) 1. Also telephone interview with Terry O'Banion, Executive Director of the League.

44 *Ironically,* Modern Maturity. "The New Senior Class," *Modern Maturity.* XXXIV (August-September, 1991), p. 26.

45 *The Association, in cooperation with the League.* Don Doucette and Catherine Ventura-Merkel, *Community College Programs for Older Adults: A Status Report.* A Joint Project of the League for Innovation in the Community College and the American Association of Retired Persons (Laguna Hills, CA: March 1991).

45 Modern Maturity *(free to members). The World Almanac and Book of Facts, 1990,* p. 363.

45 The American Association of Community Colleges (AACC) changed its name from the American Association of Community and Junior Colleges (AACJC) as of September 1, 1992. The five million number comes from an interview with James Palmer.

46 *For instance, some sixty community colleges.* "Connections." Foothill-DeAnza Community College District Newsletter (June 18, 1990), p. 9.

46 *Back in 1978.* E. L. Harlacher and J. F. Gollattscheck, "Editors' Notes," in *Implementing Community-Based Education.* New Directions for Community Colleges, No. 21 (San Francisco: Jossey-Bass, 1978), p. 7.

47   *More recently, the Commission. Building Communities*, p. 69.

Chapter 5. Teaching Today's Students

48   Page Smith, *Killing the Spirit* (New York: Viking Penguin 1990), pp. 19–20.

49   *In 1986, 110,909 full-time. Building Communities: A Vision for a New Century, A Report of the Commission on the Future of Community Colleges* (Washington D. C.: *AACJC,* 1988) pp. 12–13.

53   *A recent study reports.* Marybelle C. Keim, "Two-Year College Faculty: A Research Update," *Community College Review* XVII (Winter 1989), 38.

56   *Some twenty-five percent of the non-occupational faculty.* Keim, pp. 37, 38.

56   *But in community colleges, this commitment.* Carnegie Foundation for the Advancement of Teaching, "Change Trendlines," *Change* XXII (May/June 1990), 26.

56   *"Clarity of Commitment."* Carnegie Foundation, 26.

56   *When the Carnegie Foundation.* Carnegie Foundation, 25.

57   *Another bit of evidence.* George Riday, Ronald Bingham and Thomas Harvey, "Satisfaction of Community College Faculty: Exploding a Myth," *Community College Review,* XII (Winter 1984-85), 46–50.

57   *For part-time faculty.* Keim, p. 38.

58   *Around sixty percent. Building Communities: A Vision for a New Century,* p. 12.

58   *It is estimated that about twenty-five percent.* Lois A. Beeken, "Preface," *Proceedings from National Conference on Professional Development of Part-time Occupational Technical Faculty* (Berkeley: National Center for Research in Vocational Education, 1990), p. 1.

58   *(Although interestingly enough).* Keim, p. 39.

59   *At the very least. Building Communities: A Vision for a New Century,* p. 13.

62 *Powerful advocates for academic newcomers.* Glynda Hull and Mike Rose, "'This Wooden Shack': The Logic of an Unconventional Reading," *College Composition and Communication*, XLI (October 1990), 296–297.

64 *Her most recent project.* K. Patricia Cross and Thomas A. Angelo, *Classroom Assessment Techniques* (Board of Regents of The University of Michigan, for the National Center for Research to Improve Postsecondary Teaching and Learning, 1988), p. 1. A revised and expanded edition was published by Jossey-Bass in 1993.

64 *A key assumption.* Cross and Angelo, p. 2.

Chapter 6. Initiating the Uninitiated: The Uses of Language

66 *K. Patricia Cross, 1984.* "The Rising Tide of School Reform Reports," *Phi Delta Kappan*, 66 (November 1984), p. 170.

66 *Smokey Wilson, 1994.* "What Happened to Darleen? Reconstructing the Life and Schooling of an Underprepared Learner," in *The Community College in the Twenty-First Century*, ed. Mark Reynolds (NCTE in press).

67 *In the 1970s, Mina Shaughnessy.* Mina P. Shaughnessy, *Errors and Expectations* (New York: Oxford University Press, 1977), p. 2.

67 *Here, Shaughnessy tells us.* Shaughnessy, pp. 2–3.

68 *In her book,* Lost in Translation: A Life in a New Language (New York: Penguin Books, 1989), pp. 106–107.

71 *Puente is designed as a language based program.* From informational sheet, "Puente at a Glance."

72 *Mike Rose describes.* Mike Rose, *Lives on the Boundary* (New York: Penguin Books, 1989), pp. 44, 45.

73 *Here are adult applications.* See the chapter, "The Inspiration of Vygotsky" in Jerome Bruner's *Actual Minds,*

Possible Worlds (Cambridge: Harvard University Press, 1986). Quoted material from pages 75–76.

73 *Jerome Bruner puts this in a slightly different way.* Bruner, p. 76.

74 *". . . become increasingly adept at."* Bruner, p. 109.

75 *A recent study on vocational education.* Paula M. Hudin, et al., *Meeting the Personnel Needs of the Health Care Industry through Vocational Education Programs* (Berkeley, CA: National Center for Research in Vocational Education, University of California, 1992), pp. ix–x.

75 *In the closing paragraphs of her book.* Shaughnessy, pp. 293–294.

76 *Janet Emig, a colleague of Shaughnessy.* Janet Emig, "Mina Pendo Shaughnessy," *College Composition and Communication*. XXX (February, 1979), p. 37.

Chapter 7. Educating a Vital Workforce

78 *Peter Drucker.* Cited in Roger J. Vaughan, *New Limits To Growth: Economic Transformation and Occupational Education* (Berkeley, CA: National Center for Research in Vocational Education, University of California, 1989). p. 7.

78 *Only one out of four workers.* Vaughan, *New Limits to Growth*, pp. vii, 9.

79 *"Entry to three out of four jobs."* *Building Communities*, p. 20.

79 *"In recent years."* "Youths Lack Training for Blue-Collar Jobs, Commission Says," *The Washington Post*, reprinted in *San Francisco Chronicle* (July 3, 1991), p. 2.

79 *". . . more than half of our young people."* *What Work Requires of Schools: a SCANS Report for America 2000.* (Washington D.C.: The Secretary's Commission on Achieving Necessary Skills, U.S. Department of Labor, June 1991), p. v.

79 *More than seven out of ten technicians.* Vaughan, *New Limits to Growth*, p. 9.

80 *"Mass production techniques."* Roger J. Vaughan, "The New Limits to Growth: Economic Transformation and Vocational Education," *Phi Delta Kappan* 72 (February 1991), p. 447.

80 *There are eighteen million businesses. The Economist* (Jan. 21, 1989), p.67.

81 *Some community colleges offer one hundred.* Cohen and Brawer, p. 207.

82 *Clifford Adelman directed. The Way We Are: The Community College as American Thermometer* (Washington D.C. U.S. Government Printing Office, 1992), p. 37.

83 *And what has been happening.* Interview with Alison Bernstein, April 18, 1989.

85 *In Kansas, Johnson County Community College.* Gregory Goodwin, ed., *Celebrating Two Decades of Innovation* (Laguna Hills, CA.: The League for Innovation, 1988), p. 50, and telephone interviews with Ken Gibbon, JCCC Dean of Instruction and Edward Butt, Director of Technical Training, Burlington Northern, June 1993.

86 *St. Louis Community College.* Interview with Dale Parnell, former President, American Association of Community and Junior Colleges, April 13, 1989.

86 *When Patricia Anne Revis' sewing plant.* Prize-winning essay, reprinted in a press release of North Carolinians for Community Colleges, Winston-Salem, N.C. (April 11, 1991).

86 *New partnerships.* William E. Schmidt, "Community Colleges Emerge as Centers for Job Training," *The New York Times* (June 20, 1988), p. 1.

87 *In the* New York Times *article. Schmidt, p. A9.*

87 *The report put out.* SCANS Report (1991), pp. xvii, xviii.

90 *In our own area of California.* John Eckhouse, "Corporations Turn to the Classroom," *The San Francisco Chronicle,* (March 20, 1991), p. C–1.

91 *Some ninety-four percent of public community colleges.* Robert Lynch, James C. Palmer, W. Norton Grubb, *Community*

College Involvement in Contract Training and Other Economic Development Activities (Berkeley, CA: National Center for Research in Vocational Education, October 1991), p.38.

91 *Here are two contract programs.* John Eckhouse, p. C-1.

92 *Employers spend thirty to forty million dollars.* Anthony P. Carnevale and Lelia J. Gainor, *The Learning Enterprise* (Washington D.C., American Society of Training and Development Institutions, 1989). But there are many estimates. According to Roger Vaughan, employers in 1985 invested $210 billion "to serve one-half the workforce—about 60 million people. This included direct spending on training programs and the wages and output forgone." Vaughan, *New Limits to Growth*, p. 4.

93 *Employers cannot fill the skills gap.* Vaughan, p. 4. Vaughan estimates that "less than 1 percent of corporate training budgets is devoted to basic skills development," p. 48.

93 *One in five American adults is functionally illiterate.* Here again, the number depends on who is reporting what. Cohen and Brawer cite an inclusive twenty million, or one in five (p. 230). But Jonathan Kozol says more than sixty million adults "read beneath conventional approximations of a solid junior high school level," adding that "approximately half of that number read at fourth grade level or below." "Sacred Words" (Unpublished; distributed 7/30/86 by the American Newspaper Association Foundation.)

94 *Add to that the total number of immigrants.* Jonathan Marshall, "Immigration Bill Triples Openings for Skilled Workers," *San Francisco Chronicle* (November 24, 1990), p. 1. Marshall reports that "the legislation set aside 110,000 slots for skilled immigrants and their families, reflecting the growing concern among policymakers that the U. S. will lose its technological edge unless it attracts more of the world's talent."

94 *"At heart, the issue of remediation."* Mike Rose, "What's Right with Remedy: A College Try," *Los Angeles Times* (April 23, 1989), part v, p. 3.

94 *Only recently the U.S. Department of Education.* Statutory changes made by the Higher Education Amendment of 1991. Public Law 102–26 enacted by Congress April 9, 1991, to be effective July 1, 1991.

95 *But according to Troy Duster.* From interview May 13, 1991.

96 *Two Plus Two Tech Prep programs.* Dale Parnell, *The Neglected Majority* (Washington D.C.: The Community College Press, 1985), p. 131.

Chapter 8. Big and Bold: Democracy's Colleges

98 *William Manning. The Key of Libberty: Shewing the Causes Why a Free Government Has Always Failed, and a Remidy Against It* (Billerica, Massachusetts: The Manning Association, 1922), p. 62.

98 *"Alternatives to Universities."* (Paris, France: Organization for Economic Co-operation and Development, 1991), p. 37.

98 *As early as 1797.* William Manning, pp. 20–21.

99 *The historian, Page Smith. Killing the Spirit* (New York: Viking Penguin, 1990), p. 20.

99 *When American Council on Education.* Atwell, *The Washington Post* (May 5, 1989), p. A16.

99 *Two-year colleges receive sparse mention.* Walter Crosby Eells, *The Junior College* (Boston: Houghton Mifflin, 1931).

99 *Many of the nearly six million students.* AACJC *Summary*, p. 11.B.1.

100 *A good illustration.* Ben H. Bagdikian, *The Media Monopoly* (Boston: Beacon Press, 1990), pp. 199–200.

104 *Here it is in 1914.* James L. Ratcliff, "Should We Forget William Rainey Harper?" *Community College Review* 13 (Spring 1986), 15.

104 *Here it is in a 1950 statement.* James Ratcliff, p. 13.

Chapter 9. Keeping the Door Open: History and Change

106   K. Patricia Cross. "Transfer: Major Mission of Community Colleges?" (Unpublished paper prepared for the Leadership 2000 Conference, July 9, 1990), pp. 3–4.

106   *In those decades. Alternatives to Universities* (Paris, France: Organisation for Economic Co-operation and Development, 1991), p. 12. The report also cites the two main political considerations that gave rise to the expansion. One was "based on the conviction of employers and policy-makers that the national output of highly-qualified manpower had to grow if the respective countries were to compete successfully on the world market in times of rapidly changing technologies. The second was that . . . post-compulsory education was . . . a civil right" (p. 13).

107   *In the United States, serious and influential support.* The two chief sources for the early history of junior colleges are Walter Crosby Eells, *The Junior College*, 1931, and Leonard V. Koos, *The Junior College Movement*, 1925. For a discussion on the beginnings of the California system, see James L. Ratcliff's paper "Anthony Caminetti, University Leaders and the 1907 California Junior College Law," presented as part of the symposium "Using Historical Analysis to Assess the Development of Two-Year Colleges" at the annual meeting of the Association for the Study of Higher Education, November 23, 1987 (unpublished). For a discussion on the beginnings in Michigan (Saginaw), Massachusetts (Springfield), and Nebraska (McCook), see James Ratcliff, "'First' Public Junior Colleges in an Age of Reform," *Journal of Higher Education* LVIII (March/April 1987), 151–80. For a discussion on the beginning in Wyoming, see James Ratcliff, "A Re-Examination of the Past: Some Origins of the 'Second Best' Notion," *Community/Junior College Quarterly*, VIII (1984), 273–284.

108 *Several factors.* See Dale Tillery and William L. Deegan, "The Evolution of Two-Year Colleges Through Four Generations," in *Renewing the American Community College* (San Francisco: Jossey-Bass, 1985), pp. 3–33.

109 *A 1937 study.* Deegan and Tillery, "The Evolution . . . " in *Renewing the American Community College*, p. 11.

109 *By 1945, 315 public junior colleges. Summary*, p. 11.A.1.

109 *Only a few decades ago.* Thomas Diener, *Growth of an American Invention; A Documentary History of the Junior and Community College Movement* (Westport, CT: Greenwood Press, 1986), p. 138.

110 *Or, as one college president put it.* The late Dr. Calvin C. Flint, who, in March 1958, became the first District Superintendent and President of Foothill College in Los Altos Hills, California. The college was to be called Foothill Junior College, but in September 1958, just as classes were starting, the Board of Trustees officially changed the name to Foothill College. See *Foothill College Application for Reaffirmation of Accreditation* (Los Altos Hills, CA., 1987), p. 15.

110 *In the four decades. Summary* (AACJC, 1991), pp. 11.A.1 and 11.B.1. Increase in colleges and students from *AACJC Summary*, pp. 11.A.1–11.B.1.

112 *The nation as a whole.* Harold Hodgkinson, "Whatever Happened to the Norman Rockwell Family?" in *The Changing American Family* (Ninth Annual Providence Journal/Brown University Public Affairs Conference, March 1–16, 1989), p. 9.

112 *By the year 2000.* Harold L. Hodgkinson, *All One System: Demographics of Education — Kindergarten Through Graduate School* (Washington D.C.: Institute for Educational Leadership, Inc., 1985), p. 7.

112 *He then adds.* Hodgkinson, "Whatever Happened," p. 7.

113 *Hodgkinson concludes.* Hodgkinson, *All One System*, pp. 3, 18.

113 *In a subsequent study.* Hodgkinson, "Whatever Happened," p. 10, citing work by Richard C. Richardson, Jr.

113 *Two strong traditions are at play here.* James L. Ratcliff's unpublished paper, "Social and Political Dimensions of the Growth of Community and Junior Colleges: An Historiographic Essay," presented at the American Educational Research Association, April 25, 1984, presents a full discussion of the interplay between ideas and social forces as it affects community colleges.

114 *"A real community demand."* James L. Ratcliff, "Should We Forget William Rainey Harper?" pp. 13–15.

114 *In 1944.* James L. Ratcliff, "A Re-examination of the Past: Some Origins of the 'Second Best' Notion," *Community/Junior College Quarterly* VIII (1984), p. 279.

114 *President Ray Lyman Wilbur.* Walter Crosby Eells, p. 49.

115 *When David Starr Jordan.* James L. Ratcliff, "Anthony Caminetti, University Leaders, and the 1907 California Junior College Law," pp. 6, 11.

115 *One community college critic.* L. Steven Zwerling, "The Miami-Dade Story: Is It Really Number One?" *Change,* XX (Jan/Feb 1988), 10–23.

Chapter 10. Community College Issues: What Is Success?

117 *David Mullen.* From interview.

118 *Henry Louis Gates, Jr.* This was at Potomac State College, a community college branch of West Virginia StateUniversity. Gates described the experience in his 1992 commencement address at Borough of Manhattan Community College in New York City. Elise Raynor, "Harvard Scholar Recalls Community College Roots," *The Community, Technical, and Junior College Times* IV (August 25, 1992), 8.

119 *With public four-year institutions.* "Public Colleges, Battered by Recession, Turn Away Thousands of Students," *The Chronicle of Higher Education* XXXVIII (November 13, 1991), pp. A1, A32.

119 *Florida and North Carolina. Ibid.*

119 *California . . . is limiting. Assembly Bill #1725*, 1988. p. 3.

121 *Darrel Clowes and Bernard Levin.* "Community, Technical, and Junior Colleges: Are They Leaving Higher Education?" *Journal of Higher Education*, LX (May/June 1989), 349–55.

121 *Another audible group for change.* See, for example, Steven Brint and Jerome Karabel, *The Diverted Dream: Community Colleges and the Promise of Educational Opportunity in America, 1900–1985* (New York: Oxford University Press, 1989).

122 *As one such critic put it.* Richard C. Richardson, Jr., "The Presence of Access and the Pursuit of Achievement," in *Colleges of Choice*, ed. Judith S. Eaton (New York: American Council on Education-Macmillan Publishing Company, 1988), p. 43.

122 *Arthur Cohen and Florence Brawer point out.* Cohen and Brawer, p. 357.

122 *They argue that.* Cohen and Brawer, p. 352.

123 *A fairly low percentage.* A 1986 national survey by the Center for the Study of Community Colleges found that thirty-six percent seek transfer; thirty-four percent, job entry skills; sixteen percent, job upgrading; fifteen percent, personal interest. Other data report that eighty-six percent of entering freshmen at community colleges and eighty-one percent of freshmen at four-year colleges and universities noted "get a better job" as a very important reason for deciding to go to college. Cohen and Brawer, *The American Community College*, Second Edition (San Francisco: Jossey Bass Publishers, 1989), p. 49.

123 *Patricia Cross notes.* "Determining Missions and Priorities for the Fifth Generation," in *Renewing the American Community College* (San Francisco: Jossey-Bass, 1985), p. 257.

124 *Cohen and Brawer confirm that.* Cohen and Brawer, p. 52.

125 *In California. California Postsecondary Education Commission Student Profiles, Student Profile 5-11*, October 1990; Student Profile 5–11, December 1991.

125 *Similar numbers are reported.* James C. Palmer, "Transfer Success Confirmed in Washington State Study," *The Community, Technical, and Junior College Times* I (March 14, 1989), p. 1.

125 *At Arizona State University.* A.G. de los Santos and I. West, "Community College and University Student Transfers," *Educational Record*, 70 (Summer/Fall 1989), 82–84.

125 *In Florida.* Richard C. Richardson, Jr., and Louis W. Bender, *Students in Urban Settings: Achieving the Baccalaureate Degree*, ASHE-ERIC Higher Education Report No. 6 (Washington D.C.: Association for the Study of Higher Education, 1985), p. 5.

126 *A frequently cited study.* See, for example, Cohen and Brawer, pp. 54, 347. The original study is by A.W. Astin, *Four Critical Years: Effects of College on Beliefs, Attitudes, and Knowledge* (San Francisco: Jossey-Bass, 1977).

127 *There is confirming evidence.* Cohen and Brawer, p. 187. See also Virginia B. Smith and Alison R. Bernstein, *The Impersonal Campus: Options for Reorganizing Colleges to Increase Student Involvement, Learning and Development* (San Francisco: Jossey Bass Publishers, 1979).

127 *This is surprisingly true.* Hard data on a national trend are — no surprise — hard to come by, according to James C. Palmer, former Director of Data Collection and Policy Analysis, AACJC. Much of it is anecdotal, he told us in a 1989 interview. But a study by the Illinois

Community College Board indicates that as many as fifteen percent of their so-called "terminal" vocational students transfer to four-year colleges. Alison Bernstein of the Ford Foundation told us that the Foundation has been monitoring the transfer function for a long time and that of the students who are transferring now, a rising proportion transfer out of the so-called terminal tracks, "which in some ways throws the big lie on the difference between socalled transfer education and terminal degree education."

129 *John Losak, Dean of Institutional Research.* "What Constitutes Student Success in the Community College?" *Community College Journal for Research and Planning* (Fall/Winter 1986–87).

129 *A recent study by the Educational Testing Service. Performance at the Top: From Elementary through Graduate School* (Princeton, NJ: Educational Testing Service, 1991), p. 31.

129 *In the words of McCabe.* "The Educational Program of the American Community Colleges: A Transition," in *Colleges of Choice*, ed. Judith Eaton (ACE/Macmillan, 1988), p. 93.

129 *Community colleges do not ignore. Statistical Abstract of the United States 1991*, tables 223, 224, 225.

129 *And even with a dramatic growth.* Dale Parnell, *The Neglected Majority* (Washington D.C.: The Community College Press, 1985), p. 4.

130 *Faculty and staff seem to agree.* A recent study reported that community college "faculty and staff viewed the primary curriculum objective for the general student population as a combination of technical, liberal arts, and life skills education. . . . Only 2% viewed transfer and baccalaureate degree completion as the single most important indicator of success." Richard L. Alfred and Russell O. Peterson, "Keeping Transfer in Perspective," *AACJC JOURNAL* (June/July 1990), pp. 27–30.

List of Persons Interviewed

All interviews took place between 1988 and 1993. Affiliation/ title/identification are those at the time of the interview.

Acebo, Sandra. *Dean, Los Medanos College; currently, Dean, DeAnza College.*

Anderson, Keith. *Student.*

Bernstein, Alison. *Ford Foundation.*

Briden, Mary. *Dean, Phoenix College.*

Brown, Connie. *Student.*

Butt, Edward. *Director of Technical Training, Burlington Northern Railroad. (telephone)*

Cross, K. Patricia. *Professor, University of California, Berkeley.*

Dashiell, Margot. *Faculty, Laney College.*

Day, Mary. *Institutional Research Specialist, Maricopa District.*

DeBolt, Paul. *Faculty, Contra Costa College.*

Dobelle, Evan. *President/Chancellor, City College of San Francisco.*

Doherty, Joe. *Student.*

Donovan, Dick. *Director, Networks. Bronx Community College and Miami-Dade Community College District. (telephone)*

Duster, Troy. *Professor, University of California, Berkeley.*

Elsner, Paul. *Chancellor, Maricopa Community College District.*

Fong, Bernadine Chuck. *Dean, Foothill College.*

Forman, Susan. *Faculty, Bronx Community College.*

Galaviz, Felix. *Counselor, Puente Project.*

Gibbon, Ken. *Dean of Instruction, Johnson County Community College. (telephone)*

Harrison, Myrna. *President, Phoenix College.*

Healy, Mary K. *Research and Training Director, Puente Project; currently Director of English Credential Program, UC Berkeley.*

Hoachlander, E. Gareth. *Public Policy Analyst.*

Jordan, Nancy. *Assistant to Chancellor, Maricopa Community College District.*

Kendall, Anna. *Student.*

Lieberman, Janet. *Director of the Council of Articulated Settings, LaGuardia Community College. (telephone)*

McCabe, Robert. *President, Miami-Dade College.*

Maia, Julie. *Student; Tutor; Faculty, West Valley College.*

McGrath, Pat. *Faculty, Puente Project.*

Michalowski, Linda. *California Community College State Chancellor's Office. (telephone)*

Mitchell, Fred. *Administrator, Madison Area Technical College.*

Montgomery, Kathryn. *Student.*

Mullen, David. *Student; Tutor.*

Oberst, James Edward. *Student.*

Palmer, James C. *Director of Data Collection and Policy Analysis, AACJC.*

Parnell, Dale. *President, American Association of Community and Junior Colleges.*

Raines, Helon Howell. *Faculty, Casper College.*

Rezendes, Carmen. *Faculty, Laney College.*

Sage, George. *Faculty, Chabot College.*

Schaeffer, Lynn. *Student.*

Shanker, Joseph. *President, LaGuardia Community College.*

Sherkow, Sara. *Dean, Madison Area Technical College.*

Skinner, Byron. *President, San Jose City College.*

Smith, Linda. *Director of Research & Development, Phoenix College.*

Smith, Marvell. *Program Director, Miami-Dade Community College District.*

Wanless, Lyle D. *Dean, Madison Area Technical College.*

Watson, Carol. *Faculty, North Iowa Area Community College.*

Wall, Phil. *Faculty, Santa Monica College.*

Works Cited

Adelman, Clifford. 1992. *The Way We Are: the Community College as American Thermometer*. Washington, D.C.: U. S. Government Printing Office.

Alfred, Richard L., and Russell O. Peterson. June/July 1990. "Keeping Transfer in Perspective." *AACJC JOURNAL.* 27–30.

American Association of Community and Junior Colleges. 1991. *A Summary of Selected National Data Pertaining to Community, Technical and Junior Colleges.* Washington, D.C.: AACJC.

American Association of Community Colleges. 1992. "Statistical Brief." *Annual Fall Surveys, Full-time and Part-time Enrollments, Fall 1980–Fall 1991.* Washington, D.C.: AACC.

Astin, A. W. 1977. *Four Critical Years: Effects of College on Beliefs, Attitudes, and Knowledge.* San Francisco: Jossey-Bass.

Bagdikian, Ben H. 1990. *The Media Monopoly.* 3rd ed. Boston: Beacon Press.

Bateson, Mary Catherine. 1989. *Composing a Life.* New York: The Atlantic Monthly Press.

Beeken, Lois A. 1990. "Preface." *Proceedings from National Conference on Professional Development of Part-time Occupational Technical Faculty.* Berkeley, CA: National Center for Research in Vocational Education.

Bloom, Allan. 1987. *The Closing of the American Mind: How Higher Education Has Failed Democracy and Impoverished the Souls of Today's Students.* New York: Simon and Schuster.

Blumenstyk, Goldie. November 13, 1991. "Public Colleges, Battered by Recession, Turn Away Thousands of Students." *Chronicle of Higher Education XXXVIII: A1, A32.*

Brint, Steven, and Jerome Karabel. 1989.*The Diverted Dream: Community Colleges and the Promise of Educational Opportunity in America, 1900–1985.* New York: Oxford University Press.

Bruner, Jerome. 1986. *Actual Minds, Possible Worlds.* Cambridge, MA: Harvard University Press.

California Postsecondary Education Commission. 1990. *Student Profiles, 1990: The First in a Series of Annual Fact Books about Student Participation in California Higher Education.* No. 90–23. Sacramento, CA.

———. 1992. *Student Profiles, 1991: The Second in a Series of Annual Fact Books about Student Participation in California Higher Education.* No. 92–10. Sacramento, CA.

Carnegie Foundation for the Advancement of Teaching. May/June 1990. "Change Trendlines." *Change XXII: 23–26.*

Carnevale, Anthony P., and Lelia J. Gainor. 1989. *The Learning Enterprise.* Washington, D.C.: American Society of Training Development Institutions.

Chronicle of Higher Education. August 26, 1992. *Almanac XXXIX: No. 1.*

Clowes, Darrel, and Bernard Levin. May/June 1989. "Community, Technical, and Junior Colleges: Are They Leaving Higher Education?," *Journal of Higher Education LX: 349–355.*

Cohen, Arthur M., and Florence B. Brawer. 1989. *The American Community College.* 2nd ed. San Francisco: Jossey-Bass.

Commission on the Future of Community Colleges. 1988. *Building Communities: A Vision of a New Century.* Washington, D.C.: American Association of Community and Junior Colleges.

Cross, K. Patricia. November 1984. "The Rising Tide of School Reform Reports." *Phi Delta Kappan* 66: 167–172.

———. 1985. "Determining Missions and Priorities for the Fifth Generation." In *Renewing the American Community College*, edited by William L. Deegan and Dale Tillery. San Francisco: Jossey-Bass.

———. July 9, 1990. "Transfer: Major Mission of Community Colleges?" Unpublished paper prepared for the Leadership 2000 Conference in San Francisco.

Cross, K. Patricia, and Thomas A. Angelo. 1988. *Classroom Assessment Techniques.* Board of Regents of The University of Michigan, for the National Center for Research to Improve Postsecondary Teaching and Learning.

De los Santos, A. G., and I. West. Summer/Fall 1989. "Community College and University Student Transfers." *Educational Record* 70: 82–84.

Diener, Thomas. 1989. *Growth of an American Invention: A Documentary History of Junior and Community Colleges.* New York: Greenwood Press.

Doucette, Don, and Catherine Ventura-Merkel. March 1991. *Community College Programs for Older Adults: A Status Report.* Laguna Hills, CA: A Joint Project of the League for Innovation in the Community College and the American Association of Retired Persons.

Educational Testing Service. 1991. *Performance at the Top: From Elementary Through Graduate School.* Princeton, NJ.

Eells, Walter Crosby. 1931. *The Junior College.* Boston: Houghton Mifflin.

Emig, Janet. February 1979. "Mina Pendo Shaughnessy." *College Composition and Communication* XXX: 37–38.

Gleazer, Edmund J., Jr. 1980. *The Community College: Values, Vision, and Vitality.* Washington, D.C.: American Association of Community Colleges.

Goodwin, Gregory, ed. 1988. *Celebrating Two Decades of Innovation*. Laguna Hills, CA: League for Innovation in the Community College.

Griffith, Marlene, and Ann Connor. September 27, 1989. "To Extend Opportunities to All, Colleges Need to Redefine Remedial Education." *Chronicle of Higher Education* XXXVI: B2.

Harlacher, E. L., and J. F. Gollattscheck. *Implementing Community-Based Education*. New Directions for Community Colleges, No. 21. San Francisco: Jossey-Bass.

Hodgkinson, Harold L. 1985. *All One System: Demographics of Education — Kindergarten Through Graduate School*. Washington, D.C.: Institute for Educational Leadership.

————. 1989. "Whatever Happened to the Norman Rockwell Family?" In *The Changing American Family*. Providence, R.I.: Ninth Annual Providence Journal/Brown University Public Affairs Conference.

Hoffman, Eva. 1989. *Lost in Translation: A Life in a New Language*. New York: Penguin Books.

Hudin, Paula M., et al. 1992. *Meeting the Personnel Needs of the Health Care Industry through Vocational Education Programs*. Berkeley, CA: National Center for Research in Vocational Education.

Hull, Glynda, and Mike Rose. October 1990. "'This Wooden Shack': the Logic of an Unconventional Reading," *College Composition and Communication* XLI: 287–298.

Jaschik, Scott. November 6, 1991. "State Funds for Higher Education Drop in Year: First Decline Since Survey Began 33 Years Ago." *Chronicle of Higher Education* XXXVIII: A1, A38.

Johnston, William B. 1987. *Workforce 2000: Work and Workers for the 21st Century*. Indianapolis: Hudson Institute.

Keim, Marybelle C. Winter 1989. "Two-Year College Faculty: A Research Update," *Community College Review XVII: 34–43*.

Koos, Leonard V. 1925. *The Junior College Movement*. Boston: Ginn.

Kozol, Jonathan, 1986. "Sacred Words." Distributed by the American Newspaper Association Foundation, 7/30/86. Unpublished.

Losak, John. Fall/Winter 1986–87. "What Constitutes Student Success in the Community College?" Miami-Dade Community College, Office of Institutional Research.

Lynch, Robert, James C. Palmer, and W. Norton Grubb. 1991. *Community College Involvement in Contract Training and Other Economic Development Activities*. Berkeley, CA: National Center for Research in Vocational Education.

Manning, William. 1797. *The Key of Libberty: Shewing the Causes Why a Free Government Has Always Failed, and a Remidy Against It*. 1922 reprint. Billerica MA: The Manning Association.

McCabe, Robert. "The Educational Program of the American Community Colleges: A Transition." in *Colleges of Choice*, edited by Judith Eaton. New York: American Council on Education — Macmillan.

Organisation for Economic Co-operation and Development. 1991. *Alternatives to Universities*. Paris, France.

Palmer, James C. March 14, 1989. "Transfer Success Confirmed in Washington State Study." *The Community, Technical, and Junior College Times* I: 1.

Parnell, Dale. 1985. *The Neglected Majority*. Washington, D.C.: Community College Press.

President's Commission on Higher Education. 1947. *Higher Education for American Democracy*. Washington, D.C.: Government Printing Office, 1947.

Ratcliff, James L. January 1978. "Small Towns, Local Control, and Community-Based Colleges." *Peabody Journal of Education* 55: 99–105.

———. 1984. "A Re-Examination of the Past: Some Origins of the 'Second Best' Notion." *Community/Junior College Quarterly* VIII: 273–284.

———. April 25, 1984. "Social and Political Dimensions of the Growth of Community and Junior Colleges: An Historiographic Essay." Paper presented at Annual Meeting of the American Educational Research Association in New Orleans, LA. Unpublished.

———. Spring 1986. "Should We Forget William Rainey Harper?" *Community College Review* 13: 12–19.

———. March/April 1987. "'First' Public Junior Colleges in an Age of Reform" *Journal of Higher Education LVIII: 151–180.*

———. November 23, 1987. "Anthony Caminetti, University Leaders and the 1907 California Junior College Law." Paper presented at symposium, "Using Historical Analysis to Assess the Development of Two-Year Colleges." Annual Meeting of the Association for the Study of Higher Education. Baltimore, MD. Unpublished.

Raynor, Elise. August 25, 1992. "Harvard Scholar Recalls Community College Roots." *The Community, Technical, and Junior College Times* IV: 8.

Richardson, Richard C., Jr., 1988. "The Presence of Access and the Pursuit of Achievement." In *Colleges of Choice,* edited by Judith S. Eaton. New York: American Council on Education – Macmillan.

Richardson, Richard C., Jr. and Louis W. Bender. 1985. *Students in Urban Settings; Achieving the Baccalaureate Degree.* ASHE-ERIC Higher Education Report No. 6. Washington, D.C.: Association for the Study of Higher Education.

Riday, George, Ronald Bingham, and Thomas Harvey. Winter 1984–85. "Satisfaction of Community College Faculty: Exploding a Myth." *Community College Review XII: 46–50.*

Rose, Mike. 1989. *Lives on the Boundary.* New York: Penguin Books.

———. April 23 1989. "What's Right with Remedy: A College Try." *Los Angeles Times.* Part V.

Santovec, Mary Lou, ed. March 1990. *Recruitment and Retention in Higher Education.* Madison, WI: Magna Publications.

Shaughnessy, Mina P. 1977. *Errors and Expectations.* New York: Oxford University Press.

Smith, Page. 1990. *Killing the Spirit.* New York: Viking Penguin.

Tillery, Dale, and William L. Deegan. 1985. "The Evolution of Two-Year Colleges Through Four Generations." In *Renewing the American Community College*, edited by Deegan and Tillery. San Francisco: Jossey-Bass.

U. S. Bureau of the Census. 1991. *Educational Attainment in the United States: March 1989 and 1988.* Current Population Reports, Series P–20, No. 451. Washington, D.C.: Government Printing Office.

———. 1991. *Statistical Abstract of the United States: 1991.* Washington, D.C.: Government Printing Office.

U. S. Department of Labor. The Secretary's Commission on Achieving Necessary Skills. June 1991. *What Work Requires of Schools: A SCANS Report for America 2000.* Washington, D.C.: Government Printing Office.

Vaughan, Roger J. 1989. *New Limits To Growth: Economic Transformation and Occupational Education.* Berkeley, CA: National Center for Research in Vocational Education.

———. February 1991. "The New Limits to Growth: Economic Transformation and Vocational Education." *Phi Delta Kappan* 72: 446–449.

Wilson, Smokey. In press. "What Happened to Darleen? Reconstructing the Life and Schooling of an Underprepared Learner." in *The Community College in the Twenty-First Century*, edited by Mark Reynolds. Urbana, IL: National Council of Teachers of English.

The World Almanac and Book of Facts 1990. 1989. New York: Newspaper Enterprise Association.

Wyss, Dennis. February 27, 1989. "American Ideas: Mandela House." *Time Magazine* V: 10–11.

Zwerling, L. Steven. January/February 1988. "The Miami-Dade Story: Is It Really Number One?" *Change* XX: 10–23.